The Essentials of
# CHINESE COOKING

# CONTENTS

| | |
|---|---|
| Preface | 1 |

| | |
|---|---|
| Chinese Vegetables | 4 |
| Dried Ingredients | 8 |
| Seasonings and Spices | 10 |
| Cutting Ingredients | 12 |
| Kitchen Utensils | 14 |

**Basic Method:**

| | |
|---|---|
| Steamed Chicken with Hot Sauce | 18 |
| Marinated Smoked Salmon and Turnips | 20 |
| Corn Chicken Soup | 22 |
| Stir-Fried Shrimp and Eggs | 24 |
| Egg Fu Yong | 25 |
| Stir-Fried Pork with Cloud-ears | 26 |
| Scrambled Eggs with Tomatoes | 27 |
| Fried Spicy Prawns | 28 |
| Deep-Fried Curried Chicken | 30 |

- All recipes are designed for four persons, unless otherwise stated.
- Scallions are more familiarly known to Australasian readers as shallots.
- Cornstarch is more familiarly known as cornflour.

# PREFACE

People throughout the world are becoming much more demanding about their food, and requests are increasing for foods which are both tasty and nutritious. I particularly prefer the dishes of the Orient, especially those of China, to meat-oriented Western dishes. Chinese dishes are delicious, easy to prepare, nutritious because of the many kinds of ingredients used, and have a wide range of variety in taste.

How did I, a Japanese, become an expert in Chinese cooking? I lived in Hong Kong for five years from 1960 to 1965, while my husband was working as a correspondent in a branch office there. During that time, I was immersed in the Chinese way of life. Under cooking experts, I studied nearly 800 recipes basic to Chinese cooking.

Since returning to Japan, I have continued to visit Hong Kong several times each year. I enjoy my encounters with new dishes, as well as traditional ones. I have also visited the Chinese mainland almost every year, enjoying the true "homecooking" which can only be relished by those who visit there. I have visited the birthplaces of many famous delicacies. Therefore, I have devoted half of my life to researching the foods of China.

I will be very happy if you find that the four factors of cooking—simple, speedy, delicious, healthful—are embodied in each of the Chinese dishes which I will introduce in this book. I hope I can make many new cooking friends all over the world through the pages of this book.

*Sumi Hatano*

Sumi Hatano

All rights reserved throughout the world.
No part of this book may be reproduced in any form
without permission in writing from the publisher.

© Copyright in Japan 1987 by Sumi Hatano
Photographs by Takehiko Takei
Book Design by Momoyo Nishimura

Published by SHUFUNOTOMO CO., LTD.
2–9, Kanda Surugadai, Chiyoda-ku, Tokyo, 101 Japan

Overseas Distributors: Japan Publications Trading Co., Ltd.
P.O. Box 5030 Tokyo International, Tokyo, Japan

Distributors:
UNITED STATES: Kodansha International/USA, Ltd.,
through Harper & Row, Publishers, Inc., 10 East 53rd
Street, New York, New York 10022.  Canada: Fitzenry &
Whiteside Ltd., 195 Allstate Parkway, Markham, Ontario
L3R 4T8.

AUSTRALIA: Bookwise International, 1 Jeanes Street,
Beverley, South Australia 5007.

ISBN: 0-87040-735-X
Printed in Japan

# The Essentials of CHINESE COOKING
## Sumi Hatano

SHUFUNOTOMO/JAPAN PUBLICATIONS

| | |
|---|---|
| Fried Chicken with Cashew Nuts | 32 |
| Roast Chicken, Chinese Style | 34 |
| Fried Pork in Thick Sauce | 36 |
| Sweet-and-Sour Pork | 38 |
| Beef in Oyster Sauce | 40 |
| Pearl Balls | 42 |
| Steamed Pork Loaf with Salmon | 44 |
| Deep-Fried Meatballs | 46 |
| Stir-Fried Lamb with Miso Paste | 48 |
| "Ma-P'o-Tou-Fu" | 50 |
| Braised Tofu with Chinese Mushrooms | 52 |
| Creamed Eggplants | 54 |
| Sautéed "Ch'ing-kêng-ts'ai" | 56 |
| Vegetable Salad, Szechuan Style | 58 |
| Pickles, Cantonese Style | 60 |
| Fried Rice with Pineapple | 62 |
| Rice Gruel with Chicken and Chinese Parsley | 64 |
| Meatball Stew | 66 |
| Spring Rolls | 68 |
| Almond Gelatin Dessert | 70 |
| Coconut Milk with Tapioca | 72 |
| Pancake with Date Paste | 74 |

**Menus for Special Occasions**

| | |
|---|---|
| Appetizers | 78, 79 |
| Dinner Party | 80, 81 |
| Simple Recipes | 82, 83 |
| Bean Curd Recipes for Health | 84, 85 |
| Noodle Recipes | 86, 87 |
| Cooking at Table | 88, 89 |
| Desserts | 90, 91 |

**Preparation and Cooking...**
**Appetizers:**

| | |
|---|---|
| Hors d'Oeuvre: | |
|    "P'i-tan" Egg Custard | 94 |
|    Braised Chinese Mushroom | 94 |
|    Vinegared Jellyfish with Cucumber | 95 |
|    Braised Prawns | 95 |
| Tossed Cucumbers | 96 |
| Fried Peanuts | 96 |

**Dinner Party:**

| | |
|---|---|
| Beef and Tomato Soup | 97 |
| Scallop Stew | 98 |
| Braised Pork with Fermented Bean Curd | 99 |
| Green Asparagus in Crabmeat Cream | 100 |
| Stir-Fried Prawns with Broccoli | 101 |

**Simple Recipes:**

| | |
|---|---|
| Braised Fish Fillets | 102 |
| Stir-Fried Bean Threads | 103 |
| Stir-Fried Beef with String Beans | 104 |
| Celery Salad | 105 |

**Bean Curd Recipes for Health:**

| | |
|---|---|
| Tofu and "P'i-tan" Egg Salad | 106 |
| Braised Tofu | 107 |
| Sautéed Tofu with Crabmeat | 108 |
| "Chiao-tzu" Toufu | 109 |

**Noodle Recipes:**

| | |
|---|---|
| Fried Noodles with Shrimp | 110 |
| Beef and Scallions with Stir-Fried Noodles | 111 |
| Stir-Fried Noodles with Cuttlefish and Vegetables | 112 |
| Roast Pork with Noodles | 113 |
| Fried Noodles with Crabmeat | 114 |

**Cooking at Table:**

| | |
|---|---|
| Mongolian Fire Pot | 115 |

**Desserts:**

| | |
|---|---|
| Sesame Seed Balls | 116 |
| Open Mouth Laughs | 117 |
| Steamed Cake | 118 |
| Useful Hints for Cooking | 119 |

# CHINESE VEGETABLES

**"Ch'ing-kêng-ts'ai"** 青梗菜
This is a vegetable about 8 in. (20 cm) long with light green leaves and stalks that turn translucent grass green when cooked. It has a rather bland taste, but is agreeably crisp. In China, it is cultivated around Shanghai and southward, and several varieties of this vegetable are to be found all the year round.

For banquets, the outer leaves are peeled off and only the hearts are used, uniformly stripped. However, for everyday meals, both the outer leaves and the hearts are used, cut into thin strips or bite-sized pieces.

This vegetable can be stir-fried with sliced beef or pork, used in stews and soups, or first stir-fried and then cooked with a little soup which is thickened with cornstarch at the last moment. It is rich in vitamin C. (1)

**"Hsiang-ts'ai"** 香菜
**(Chinese coriander)**
This herb is called Chinese parsley, and looks like parsley, but has a strong distinctive flavor. It is used to flavor shark's fin soup and to garnish deep-fried dishes and salads. In the North, it is used as one of the seasonings in the sauce for "shuan-yang-jou" (Mongolian Fire Pot).

Dried "hsiang-ts'ai" seeds are called "yuan-sui-mi" (coriander seeds). (2)

**"Jiu-huang" (Yellow scallion)** 韭黃
This vegetable is cultivated in the same way as bean sprouts, covered with straw, chaff or earthenware drain pipes to shut out the sun. It is a pale yellow, delicate-looking vegetable, but has a strong, appetizing flavor.

The green scallion is mainly used for everyday meals, but the yellow variety is more expensive and is used for dainty dishes.

Cooked with shrimps, crabmeat or chicken and covered with thickening, it can be served at banquets. Even without shrimp or crabmeat, you can make a fine vegetable dish by stir-frying "jiu-huang" with bean sprouts from which you have carefully removed the heads and the roots.

You can also enjoy the flavor of this vegetable by stir-frying it with shredded pork, using it in spring rolls or in fried bean curd sheet rolls.

It is rich in vitamins A, B$_2$ and C.　　(3)

## "Suan-tai" (Garlic sprouts) 蒜苔

Also known as "ching-suan-tai," and usually sold as a frozen vegetable, it is now available fresh even outside China.

When garlic leaves are out, budded stalks, long and straight like chopsticks, shoot up. The buds are removed and the stalks are cut down to about 10 in. (25 cm)

These stalks are naturally sweet and pleasantly crisp. Their smell, though not so sharp, is similar to that of garlic.

When you are using frozen "suan-tai," it is best to thaw and peel the stalks.

There is no need to peel fresh stalks. You can just cut them into 2 to 2 1/2-in. (5–6 cm) lengths and stir-fry them. "Suan-tai" can be cooked alone or with shredded beef, pork or mushrooms. This vegetable tastes better when seasoned with soy sauce, bean paste or oyster sauce.　　(6)

## "Ta-suan" (Garlic) 大蒜　　(9)

## "Suan-miao" (Garlic leaves) 蒜苗

"Suan-miao" is a part of the garlic leaf. While it is young, it can be stir-fried or stewed like green onions or scallions, but old garlic leaves are hard and stringy.

In Szechuan cooking, "suan-miao," cut into 1 1/2 to 2-in. (4–5 cm) lengths, is added to "ma-p'o-tou-fu" (Bean Curd and Minced Pork in Hot Bean Paste Sauce) just before serving.

## "Chiu-ts'ai (Scallion) 韭菜　　(12)

## "Chiu-ts'ai-hua" (Scallion flower)
韭菜花　　(4)

**Snow peas** (8)

### "Tou-miao" (Pea sprouts) 豆苗
This refers to the young sprouts of a variety of pea, specially improved so that the leaves are tender enough to be eaten. It is also called "wan-tou-miao." Only the upper 4 in. (10 cm) or so of the tender part of the young shoots are used for cooking.

When stir-fried, it is very tender and tasty, full of the flavor of fresh green peas. It is a high quality vegetable served more often at banquets than for everyday meals, and is often used in Shanghai, Cantonese and Szechwan cooking.

As it is used for banquets, it is generally stir-fried with crabs, shrimps or chicken and coated with thickening. However, it is also delicious when lightly stir-fried with just a pinch of salt. It is sometimes added in soups.

When stir-frying "tou-miao," you must take special care not to overcook it. It is rich in vitamin C. (10)

**Ginger root, fresh ("chiang")** 姜 (11)

**Green onion ("ta-ts'ung")** 大葱 (5)

**Mushrooms, fresh** 冬菇 (7)

### "Pak-choi" 白菜
This vegetable is cultivated in southern China and is smaller than "pai-ts'ai," which is harvested in winter in the North. Although identical Chinese characters are used to write "pak-choi" and "pai-ts'ai," they are completely different, and "pak-choi" is a southern vegetable commonly found in Canton. It is about 6 in. (15cm) long. The leaves are tender and of a darker shade than "ch'ing-kêng-ts'ai," but the stalks are crisp and white. The dark green leaves contrast beautifully with the shiny white stalks. It has a light taste and can be fried, stewed or covered with thickening after cutting into two or four pieces lengthwise. Whichever method you use, be careful not to overcook it. This vegetable is delicious when Stir-Fried with Pork, Beef or Chicken. It contains vitamin C and calcium.

# DRIED INGREDIENTS

**"Mu-erh" (Cloud ears)** 木耳
An edible fungus (Auricularia auricula-judae) which grows on dead tree bark. When fresh, it is soft and jelly-like. Its name (meaning "tree ears' in Chinese) derives from its ear-like shape.

The most common variety is the black "mu-erh." It is sold dried and must be soaked before cooking. Be careful to soak a small quantity at a time because it swells a great deal. After soaking, remove the woody part of the stems and add to stir-fried or stewed dishes, soups or salads. (1)

**"Hsia-mi" (Dreid shrimp)** 蝦米
Shelled and dried shrimp, also called "hsia-kan," "hai-mi" or "k'ai-yang."

Dried shrimp are rich in calcium and phosphorus and have a distinctive taste quite different from that of fresh shrimp.

They should be rinsed and soaked in lukewarm water before cooking. They can be stir-fried, added to steamed dishes or salads. The water used for soaking can also be used as a tasty soup stock. (2)

**"Fên-ssǔ" (Mung bean noodles),** 粉絲
**"Fên-p'i" (Mung bean sheets)** 粉皮
Fine white noodles made from the green mung bean "lü-tou." These are very firm and do not dissolve even when cooked for a fairly long period of time. These noodles can be added to soups. (3)

Another type of noodle "fen-p'i" is also made from the green mung bean. This is boiled until soft and is used in salads. (4)

**Red Chili pepper ("hung-la-chiao")**
紅辣椒 (5)

**"P'i-tan" (Thousand-year eggs)** 皮蛋
Also known as "sung-hua-tan," "p'i-tan" are duck eggs soaked in lye and preserved by coating with a mixture of clay, chaff, etc.

The coating and the shell must be removed before using. The egg whites have a gelatinous consistency, and the ones speckled with marble-like patterns are considered the best. They are generally sliced and served uncooked as hors-d'oeuvres. (6)

### "Hai-chê-p'i" (Jellyfish) 海蜇皮
This is jellyfish preserved in alum and salt. Nowadays it is usually sold shredded.

If you are using ordinary "hai-chê-p'i," soak it overnight in water, pour boiling water over it until it curls up, rinse once more in cold water and then season it.

Instant "hai-chê-p'i" is also available that does not have to be soaked overnight, but its volume diminishes when soaked and it is inferior in flavor. (7)

### "Tung-ku" (Dried Chinese black mushrooms) 冬菇
Dried mushrooms are an indispensable ingredient in Chinese cooking. The variety that is harvested in the fall and winter is called "tung-ku" (winter mushroom), and the fleshy variety with cracked caps is called "hua-ku" (flower mushroom). It is also known as "hsiang-ku" (fragrant mushroom) because of its fragrance.

To prepare mushrooms soak in water until tender, remove the woody part of the stem and use in stir-fried, stewed or steamed dishes and in soups. (8)

### Dates, red, dried ("hung-tsao") 紅棗
(9)

### "Ts'ao-ku" (Straw mushrooms) 草菇
Straw mushrooms are a kind of mushroom harvested in the spring. Boiled and canned "ts'ao-ku" is available outside China. (10)

### Kan-pei (Dried scallops) 干貝
These are the dried shell-ligaments of scallops and similar shellfish. They have a delicate taste and are suitable for use in dainty dishes. Soak until tender and add to stewed, stir-fried or steamed dishes or soups. (11)

# SEASONINGS AND SPICES

**"Chi-ma-chiang"**
**(Sesame seed paste)** 芝麻醬
"Chi-ma-chiang" is made from white sesame seeds ground into paste, and is used in sauces for steamed chicken, "shuan-yang-jou" (page 88) or salads. (1)

**"Tou-pan-chiang"**
**(Brown bean paste)** 豆瓣醬
"Tou-pan-chiang" is made from fermented lima bean paste mixed with chili peppers and other seasonings. It is a hot seasoning characteristic of Szechuan cooking. Its name (meaning "bean petal paste") is derived from the shape of the lima beans, which resemble flower petals.

In Szechuan province, people generally use ready-made paste, but the restaurants prepare their own "tou-pan-chiang." When it is not available, you can use instead "la-yu" (chili pepper oil) or Tabasco. (2)

**"Tien-mien-chiang"**
**(Sweet brown bean paste)** 甜麵醬
This is a sweet dark brown bean paste fermented with wheat flour. Also called "tien-chiang," it accompanies such delicacies as "Peking duck" and roast piglet.

It is added to stir-fried or stewed dishes, and is also used at the table. When you are using Japanese bean paste instead, add sugar and soup to "Haccho-miso" (brown bean paste), heat and stir thoroughly. (3)

**"Tou-chi"**
**(Fermented soy beans)** 豆豉
"Tou-chi" is made from black soy beans steamed and fermented with malt, flour and salt. They are like Japanese "hama-natto," a famous product of Hamamatsu, or Kyoto's "daitokuji-natto." Minced and used in stewed, stir-fried or steamed dishes, their distinctive flavor enriches the taste of the dishes. (4)

**"Fu-ju"**
**(Fermented bean curd cake)** 腐乳
Fu-ju is bean curd fermented with salt, spices and seasonings, and has a special taste and fragrance. It is also known as "chiang-tou-fu" or "nan-ju."

The white type, called "pai-fu-ju," is served as is with boiled rice or congee. The red type, called "hong-fu-ju," is mainly used as a seasoning. "Fu-ju" is also added to stir-fried or stewed dishes and to the sauce for "shuan-yang-jou." (see page 88)          (5)

**"Hao-yu"**
**(Oyster sauce)** 蠔油
Oystes Sauce is a special seasoning used only in Chinese cooking. It is made by fermenting salted oysters. A small amount added to dishes heightens the flavor. It is often used in Cantonese cooking, added to stir-fried or stewed dishes, or used as a dip for stir-fried dishes seasoned just with salt.     (6)

**"Hua-chiao"**
**(Szechuan peppercorns)** 花椒
Dried brown Szechuan peppercorns are one of the most frequently used spices in Chinese cooking. Whole peppercorns are added to stewed meat. Toasted, ground and mixed with salt, they are served with deep-fried dishes.       (7)

**"La-yu"**
**(Chili pepper oil)** 辣油
"La-yu" is a hot seasoning made by adding chili pepper to vegetable oil. It is also called "la-chiao-yu." It is mainly used at the table as a seasoning. For example, a few drops are added to soy sauce in which "Chiao-tzu" and "Shao-mai" are dipped.

It is sold in small bottles but can easily be made at home. Heat five tablespoons oil, add two or three minced chili peppers, stir-fry over low heat until the oil is well flavored, strain the oil and discard peppers.       (8)

# CUTTING INGREDIENTS
Here are a few cutting terms used in this book.

"Hsuan-tao-k'uai": Cut into rolling cubes
旋刀塊

"P'ien": Slice
片

"K'uai": Cube
塊

"Ting": Chop coarsely
丁

"Mo": Mince finely
末

"Ti'ao": Cut into sticks
條

"Tuan": Cut into thick slices or chop into random lengths
段

"Ssŭ": Cut into strips or shred
絲

# KITCHEN UTENSILS

1: hand strainer  2: Peking-Style wok  3: hand (iron) strainer  4: wok
5: ladle  6: iron spatula  7: sieve  8: bamboo strainer  9: strainer
10: tripod  11: steamer  12: whisk  13: turner  14: skimmer
15: chopsticks  16: cleaver  17: chopping board

**Basic Method:**

# Steamed Chicken with Hot Sauce

**Ingredients:**
220 g (1/2 lb.) fillet of chicken breast
　Pinch of salt
　1 tablespoon Chinese rice wine or sake
4–5 lettuce leaves
70 g (2 1/2 oz.) dried "fên-p'i" (mung bean sheet noodles)
Hot sauce:
　4 tablespoons "chih-ma-chiang" (sesame seed paste)
　2 tablespoons "tou-pan-chiang" (brown bean sauce)
　1 teaspoon peanut butter
　1 tablespoon sesame oil
　1 tablespoon chicken stock
　1 tablespoon vinegar
　2 tablespoons sugar
　1 teaspoon salt
　1/8 teaspoon pepper

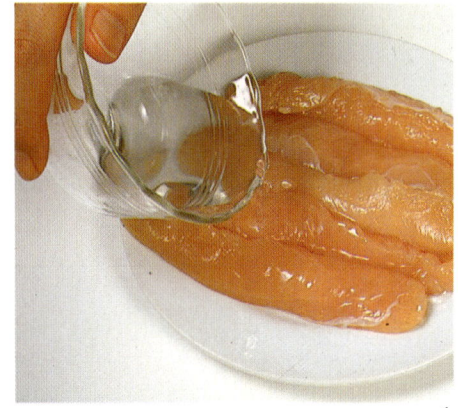
1

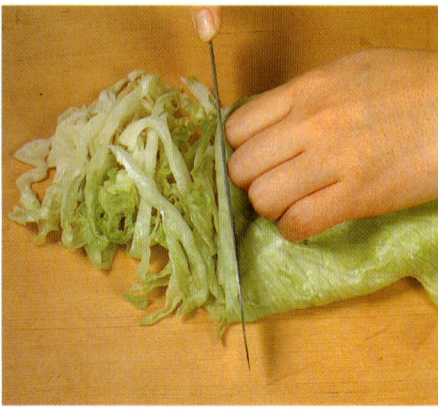
4

2

5

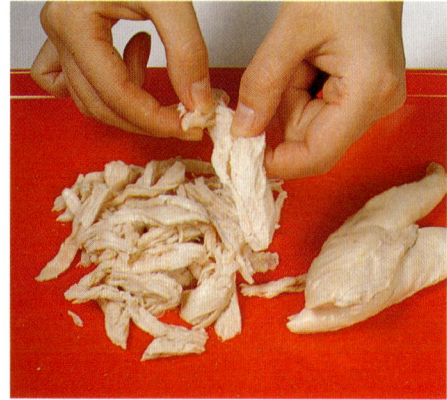
3

**Method:**
**1.** Sprinkle chicken with salt and wine, place on plate and steam for 15 minutes. When the meat is a little cool, tear it into thin strips.　　　　　(1–3)
**2.** Cut lettuce julienne.　　　　(4)
**3.** Boil "fên-p'i" until soft, soak in cold water, drain and cut into 2/3-inch (15 mm) wide pieces.　　　　　(5)
**4.** In a small bowl, mix "chih-ma-chiang" with peanut butter, add "tou-pan-chiang," sesame oil, chicken stock, vinegar, sugar, salt and pepper, and then blend well.
**5.** Arrange on plate in this order: the "fên-p'i," the lettuce and the hot sauce over the chicken.

# Marinated Smoked Salmon and Turnips

**Ingredients:**
5 turnips
100 g (3 1/2 oz.) smoked salmon
1 teaspoon salt
Vinegar mixture:
   1/2 cup vinegar
   1/3 cup sugar
   Little sesame oil
Mint leaves for garnish

**Method:**
**1.** Peel turnips, slice thinly, and sprinkle with salt. Let stand for a while, turning occasionally. (1–2)
**2.** When liquid comes out of the turnips, rinse and drain them. (3–4)
**3.** Slice smoked salmon thinly.
**4.** In a bowl combine the vinegar mixture and marinate the turnips until the flavor is absorbed. Add the smoked salmon. Place on a plate and garnish with mint leaves on top.

1

2

3

4

21

# Corn Chicken Soup

### Ingredients:
2 egg whites
4 cups chicken stock
220 g (1/2 lb.) ground chicken
1 can (240 g: 8 oz.) sweet corn
1/2 teaspoon salt
2 tablespoons cornstarch, dissolved in 4 tablespoons water
2 tablespoons minced parsley

### Method:
1. Stiffly beat egg whites in a bowl.
2. Bring chicken stock to a boil, add chicken and stir to break it up into fine pieces. Skim off the scum, and add corn and salt. Thicken with dissolved cornstarch. (1–2)
3. Bring to a boil again and quickly fold in beaten egg whites. Remove from heat. (3)
4. Pour the soup into a serving bowl and garnish with parsley.

1

2

3

# Stir-Fried Shrimp and Eggs

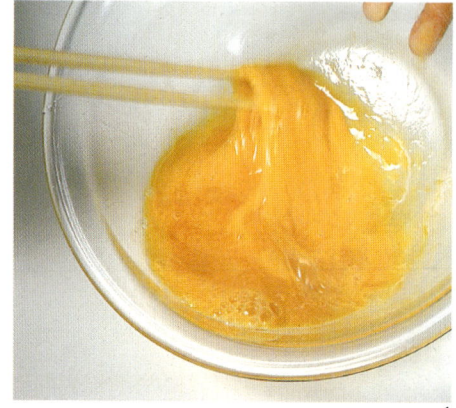
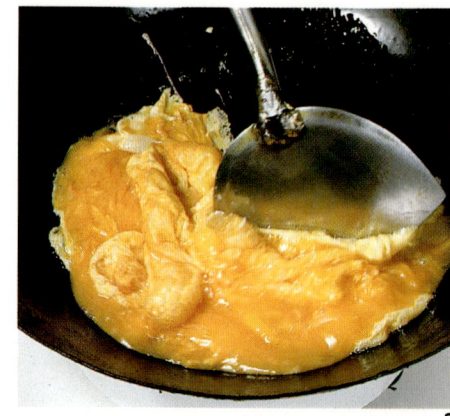

1                              2

**Ingredients:**
150 g (1/3 lb.) shrimp
  1/2 egg white*
  2 teaspoons cornstarch
8 eggs
1/2 teaspoon salt
1/2 teaspoon sugar
4 tablespoons oil
1 tablespoon Chinese rice wine or sake
Chinese parsley for garnish
3 cups oil for deep-frying

**Method:**
1. Shell the shrimp and remove the black vein. Rinse and drain.
2. Beat eggs in a mixing bowl, and add salt and sugar. Combine well. (1)
3. Mix 1/2 egg white with the shrimp, and coat the shrimp with cornstarch. Deep-fry the shrimp over medium heat.
4. Heat 4 tablespoons oil in a wok, pour in the beaten eggs. Stir over high heat. When the eggs begin to set, add the shrimp and sprinkle with wine, and stir quickly. (2)

*The egg white for coating can be taken from the 8 eggs.

# Egg Fu Yong

### Ingredients:
1 small can (93 g: 3 oz.) crabmeat
1 tablespoon Chinese rice wine or sake
2–3 dried Chinese mushrooms
100 g (3 1/2 oz.) boiled bamboo shoots
1/4 cup green peas
1/2 green onion
Mixture A:
   1 1/2 cups soup stock
   1 tablespoon soy sauce
   1 teaspoon sugar
   Dash of MSG (optional)
6 eggs
1/2 teaspoon salt
1 teaspoon cornstarch, dissolved
   in 2 teaspoons cold water
5 tablespoons oil

### Method:
**1.** Flake crabmeat and remove bones. Sprinkle with wine.
**2.** Slice bamboo shoots into 1 1/2-inch (4 cm) length thin pieces. Soak dried Chinese mushroom in water, remove stems and slice thinly. Soak peas in hot water if frozen, or pour hot water over peas if canned. Shred green onion into 1 1/2-inch (4 cm) length strips.
**3.** Combine Mixture A well.
**4.** In a bowl beat eggs, add the crabmeat and salt, and mix gently. (1)
**5.** Heat 3 tablespoons oil in a wok, turning the wok so that the sides are thoroughly greased. Pour the egg mixture into the wok over high heat. When the bottom of the egg mixture is set, turn it over with a turner several times until the surface is cooked and the inside is half set. Remove to a serving plate.
**6.** After scraping the wok with the turner, heat 2 tablespoons of fresh oil, and briefly sauté the bamboo shoots, mushroom and peas. Add Mixture A. (2) Bring to a boil and thicken with the dissolved cornstarch. Pour over the fried egg mixture.

# Stir-Fried Pork with Cloud-ears

**Ingredients:**
150 g (5 oz.) sliced pork
2 dried cloud-ears (large size)
4 eggs
   1/4 teaspoon sugar
   1/4 teaspoon salt
Mixture A:
   1 tablespoon soy sauce
   2 teaspoons sugar
   2 teaspoons cornstarch
   1 tablespoon oil
1 tablespoon Chinese rice wine or sake
1/2 teaspoon salt
2 tablespoons oil

 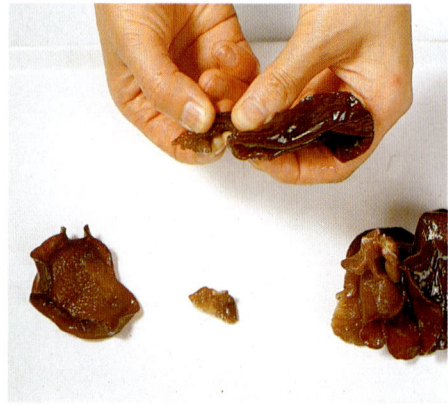

**Method:**
**1.** Cut the pork into bite-sized pieces and marinate in Mixture A.
**2.** Soak the dried cloud-ears in water, remove the stems and cut into bite-sized pieces.                                (1–2)
**3.** Beat the eggs, add 1/4 teaspoon sugar and salt. Stir-fry the eggs until half set.
**4.** In a wok heat 2 tablespoons oil, stir-fry the pork, and add the eggs and the cloud-ears. Season with wine and salt.

# Scrambled Eggs with Tomatoes

**Ingredients:**
2 ripe tomatoes
4 eggs
1 teaspoon minced garlic
Mixture A:
   2 teaspoons sugar
   1/2 teaspoon salt
   1 tablespoon soy sauce
   1 tablespoon Chinese rice wine or sake
   1 teaspoon Tabasco sauce
2 teaspoons cornstarch, dissolved in 4 teaspoons cold water
5 tablespoons oil

**Method:**
1. Wash tomatoes and remove the hard stem. Cut into bite-sized wedges. (1)
2. Beat eggs well.
3. Heat 3 tablespoons oil in a wok over high heat, pour in eggs and stir-fry until eggs begin to thicken. Remove the eggs from the pan, and set them aside.
4. Heat 2 tablespoons fresh oil in the wok and sauté the garlic. When it becomes fragrant, add the tomatoes and stir quickly. (2)
5. Add the eggs and season with Mixture A. Thicken with dissolved cornstarch.

# Fried Spicy Prawns

**Ingredients:**
12 prawns
1 teaspoon minced garlic
1 teaspoon minced fresh ginger
1 tablespoon minced green onions
1 tablespoon Chinese rice wine or sake
1/2 teaspoon salt
1 teaspoon soy sauce
1 tablespoon tomato ketchup
1 tablespoon "tou-pan-chiang"
   (brown bean sauce)
2 tablespoons oil
2 cups oil for frying

**Method:**
1. Remove the pleopod and legs of the prawns with scissors, slit the back and remove the black veins. Cut prawns into two or three pieces. Wipe off thoroughly. (1–3)
2. Heat 2 cups oil in a wok and fry prawns until they turn red. Remove prawns from the pan and set aside. Remove the oil from the wok. (4–5)
3. Heat 2 tablespoons fresh oil in the same wok and sauté garlic, ginger and green onion. When they become fragrant, add tomato ketchup and "tou-pan-chiang." Add the prawns and sprinkle with wine, salt and soy sauce, stirring quickly over high heat. (6–7)

# Deep-Fried Curried Chicken

### Ingredients:
800 g (1 3/4 lb.) chicken breast
　with bone, cut into chunks
Seasoning:
　1 teaspoon sugar
　1/2 teaspoon salt
　2 tablespoons soy sauce
　2 teaspoons curry powder
　1 tablespoon Chinese rice wine or
　　sake
Watercress for garnish
6 cups oil for deep-frying

### Method:
**1.** In a bowl, place chicken and add seasoning ingredients. Combine and marinate for 30 to 60 minutes. (1–3)
**2.** Wipe the chicken with a cloth or paper towel. Heat 6 cups oil in a wok. Add the chicken and deep-fry over medium heat until well cooked. (4–6)
**3.** Place the chicken on a plate and garnish with watercress.

1

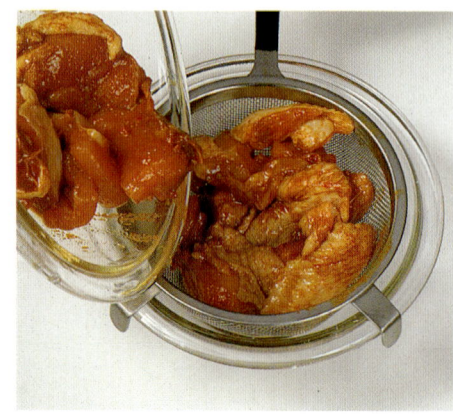
4

2

5

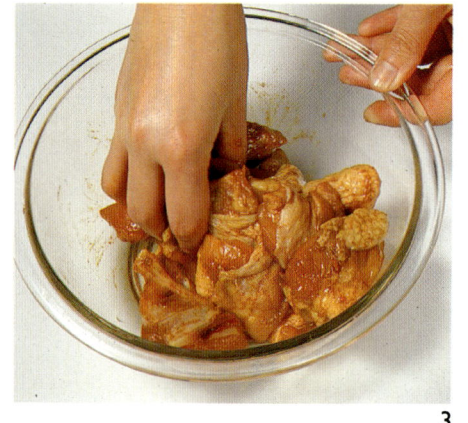
3

6

# Fried Chicken with Cashew Nuts

**Ingredients:**
800 g (about 2 lb.) chicken, boned
Mixture A:
   5 tablespoons soy sauce
   2 tablespoons Chinese rice wine
     or sake
   1 tablespoon sugar
   Dash of pepper
   1 tablespoon ginger juice
100 g (3 1/2 oz.) cashew nuts
1/2 green onion for garnish
6 cups oil

**Method:**
1. Cut the chicken into 2/3-inch (16 mm) cubes. (1)
2. Cut the green onion julienne style and soak in water for a while. Drain. (2)
3. Combine mixture A in a bowl and marinate the chicken in the mixture for 30 minutes (3). Drain and wipe off with a cloth or paper towel. (4)
4. Heat 6 cups of oil over medium heat and deep-fry the chicken until done. (5)
5. Fry the cashew nuts in deep oil over high heat until light brown. (6)
6. Place the chicken and the cashew nuts on a plate and garnish with the julienned green onion sprinkled on top.

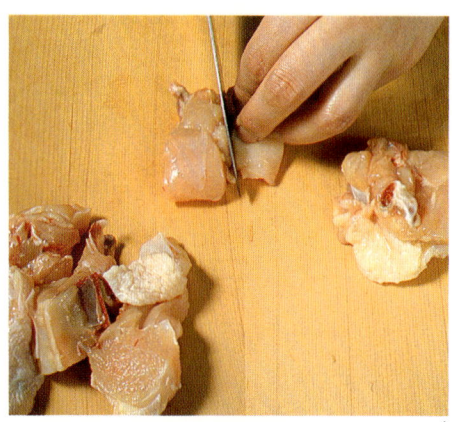
1

3

2

5

3

6

# Roast Chicken, Chinese Style

**Ingredients:**
2 chicken thighs, bones
1/4 leek, pounded
1 clove fresh ginger, pounded
Mixture A:
   1 teaspoon ginger juice
   3 tablespoons soy sauce
   1 tablespoon Chinese rice wine or sake
   1 tablespoon sugar
1 tablespoon cornstarch
Mixture B:
   1 tablespoon "tien-mien-chiang" (sweet brown bean paste)
   1 teaspoon sugar
Dash of salt mixed with powdered Szechuan peppercorns
2 tablespoons oil

**Method:**
**1.** Cut out the tendons of the chicken and marinate it in Mixture A with the leek and fresh ginger. Before frying the chicken, rub with cornstarch. (1–2)
**2.** In a wok heat 2 tablespoons oil and fry the chicken with the skin side down over medium heat. When the skin becomes light brown, turn the chicken over, cover it with a lid and cook over low heat until well cooked. (3–4)
**3.** Combine Mixture B thoroughly. Before turning off the heat, brush the chicken with Mixture B. Cut the chicken into bite-sized pieces. Place lettuce on a serving plate, put the chicken on top and sprinkle with salt mixed with powdered Szechuan peppercorns.

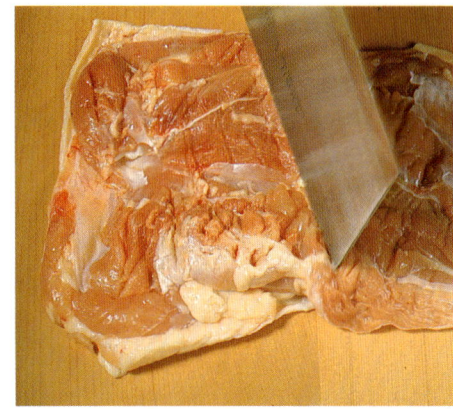
1
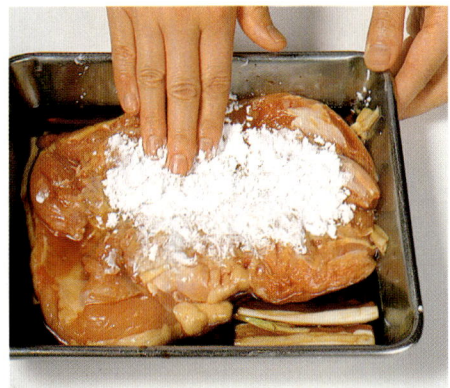
2

3

4

# Fried Pork in Thick Sauce

1

**Ingredients:**
800 g (2 lb.) pork, chuck roast
1 egg, beaten
Cornstarch for coating
1 teaspoon minced garlic
Mixture A:
   1/2 cup soup stock
   2 1/2 tablespoons soy sauce
   1 1/2 tablespoons sugar
   1 tablespoon Chinese rice wine
    or sake
1 bunch of spinach
   1 cup water
1 teaspoon salt
6 cups oil for deep-frying
4 tablespoons oil

2

**Method:**
**1.** Pound the pork thoroughly and cut into bite-sized pieces.
**2.** Combine Mixture A well.
**3.** Coat the pork with beaten egg and then with cornstarch. Heat 6 cups of oil over high heat and deep-fry the pork until done. (1–2)
**4.** In a wok heat 2 tablespoons oil over high heat, sauté the garlic and add the deep-fried pork. Season with Mixture A and stir-fry. Set aside.
**5.** Wash the spinach thoroughly without cutting, and stir-fry in 2 tablespoons oil over high heat (3). Add salt and water, cover with a lid and cook until soft. Drain and place on a serving plate.
**6.** Place the pork on top.

3

# Sweet-and-Sour Pork

**Ingredients:**
350 g (3/4 lb.) lean pork
2 green peppers, or sweet red peppers
5 slices pineapple
1 dried hot red pepper
2 green onions
1 egg
1 tablespoon minced garlic
Sauce Mixture:
    1/4 cup vinegar
    4 1/2 tablespoons sugar
    1/2 teaspoon salt
    1 tablespoon tomato ketchup
    2 tablespoons Worcestershire sauce
    1 tablespoon Chinese rice wine
      or sake
2 teaspoons cornstarch, dissolved
  in 4 teaspoons water
Cornstarch for coating
2 tablespoons oil
6 cups oil for deep-frying

**Method:**
**1.** Cut pork into 1/3-inch (1 cm) thick slices, lightly pound with the dull edge of a knife, and cut into bite-sized pieces. (1–2)
**2.** Cut the green peppers lengthwise, remove the seeds and stems, and cut into bite-sized pieces. Cut pineapple into bite-sized pieces.
**3.** Seed the red pepper and cut in round slices. Cut green onions into 12 lengths. (3)
**4.** Beat egg. Dip the pieces of pork in the beaten egg and roll them over in the cornstarch.
**5.** Heat 6 cups oil in a wok, and deep-fry the pork until light brown. Remove the oil from the wok.
**6.** Heat 2 tablespoons of fresh oil in a wok. Quickly sauté the garlic and green onions over high heat, and add the red pepper. Then add the other ingredients in this order; green peppers, pineapple and pork.
**7.** Blend the Sauce Mixture, pour in the sauce, and stir briefly. Thicken with dissolved cornstarch.

1

2

3

# Beef in Oyster Sauce

**Ingredients:**
450 g (1 lb.) beef fillet
1 egg white
1 teaspoon cornstarch
Sauce Mixture:
   2 tablespoons soup stock
   3 tablespoons oyster sauce
   1 teaspoon sugar
   1 tablespoon soy sauce
   Dash of pepper
1 teaspoon minced garlic
1 teaspoon minced ginger
1 tablespoon minced green onion
1 cup water
1 tablespoon Chinese rice wine or sake
1 teaspoon cornstarch, dissolved
   in 2 teaspoons cold water
1 tomato
Parsley
4 tablespoons oil
6 cups oil for deep-frying

**Method:**
**1.** Cut the beef into bite-sized pieces. Combine the Sauce Mixture well. (1)
**2.** Put the beef in a bowl and mix with the egg white and cornstarch with your hands. (2)
**3.** Heat 6 cups oil in a wok over medium-low heat. Add the beef and quickly deep-fry for 1–2 minutes.
**4.** Wash the tomato and cut in half then slice.
**5.** Clean the wok. Heat 2 tablespoons oil and sauté the garlic, green onion and ginger. When it becomes fragrant, add the beef and sprinkle with wine. (3)
**6.** Add the Sauce Mixture, quickly sauté, and thicken with dissolved cornstarch (4). Quickly spoon on a plate and garnish with tomato slices. Arrange with parsley.

1

2

3

4

# Pearl Balls

**Ingredients:**
1 cup glutinous rice
Seasonings for rice:
   1/2 teaspoon sugar
   1/2 teaspoon salt
450 g (1 lb.) ground chicken
Seasonings for chicken:
   1 tablespoon Chinese rice wine
     or sake
   1 1/2 teaspoons salt
   1 tablespoon sugar
   Water

**Method:**
**1.** Rinse rice thoroughly and soak in water overnight. (1)
**2.** With a knife or food processor, mince the ground chicken to get a smooth texture.
**3.** Combine the chicken and seasonings in a bowl. Shape the chicken mixture into 1-inch (2.5 cm) balls. (2–3)
**4.** Drain the rice and mix with seasonings. (4)
**5.** Roll meatballs in rice. Place meatballs in steamer leaving some space between each one. Put lid on and steam over medium heat for 20 minutes. (5–6)
**6.** Serve hot. If meatballs get cool, steam them again.

1

4

2

5

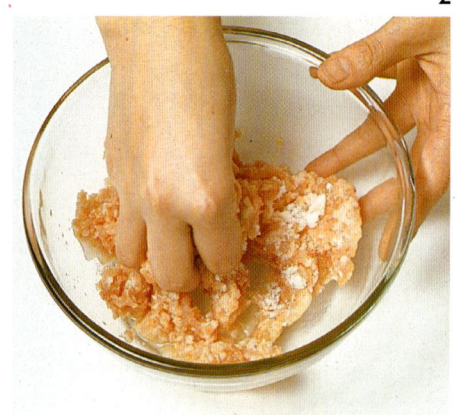
3

6

43

# Steamed Pork Loaf with Salmon

**Ingredients:**
400 g (1 lb.) ground pork
2 eggs
2 slices of slightly-salted salmon
Mixture A:
    1/2 egg white
    1/2 teaspoon sugar
    1/8 teaspoon salt
    2 tablespoons soup stock
    1 tablespoon Chinese rice wine or sake
1 cup soup stock
1 teaspoon cornstarch dissolved in
    2 teaspoons water
Lettuce leaves

1

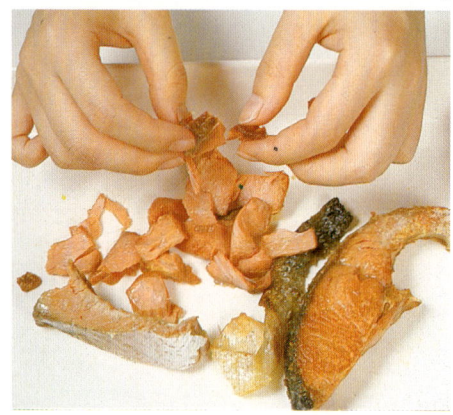

2

3

**Method:**
**1.** Chop the ground pork well with the sharp edge of a knife or in a food processor.
**2.** Hardboil the eggs, shell them, and cut them crosswise into slices.
**3.** Grill the salmon, remove the bones and skin, and flake into pieces. (1–2)
**4.** Mix the ground pork and the salmon in a bowl. Add Mixture A and knead well.
**5.** Lightly oil a bowl with lard, arrange the egg slices close together on the bottom of the bowl in a single layer, and then cover the eggs with the pork mixture (3). Preheat a steamer over medium heat. Place the bowl in the steamer and steam for 20–25 minutes. Take the bowl out of the steamer and invert over a serving plate.
**6.** In a small pan bring soup stock to a boil, thicken with dissolved cornstarch and pour over the loaf.
**7.** Garnish with lettuce leaves.

# Deep-Fried Meatballs

**Ingredients:**
300 g (3/4 lb.) ground beef
1/4 green onion
1 slice of fresh ginger
1/2 cup water
Seasonings for Meatballs:
   1 tablespoon sugar
   1 tablespoon cornstarch
   1/2 teaspoon salt
   1/2 teaspoon soy sauce
   Little sesame oil
   Little pepper
   MSG (optional)
1 bunch of watercress
Szechuan peppercorns salt
6 cups oil for deep-frying

**Method:**
1. Pound ground beef with the blunt side of a Chinese cleaver. (1)
2. Shred green onion and ginger and soak in 1/2 cup water for 20 minutes to season the water. Remove the green onion and ginger, and set the seasoned water aside.
3. Combine the ground beef and seasonings in a bowl. Add the seasoned water and mix well with hands. (2–3)
4. Shape the beef mixture into 1-inch (2.5 cm) balls. (4)
5. Heat 6 cups oil in a wok. Add meatballs and deep-fry over low heat, turning occasionally, until light brown and well cooked. Fry the meatballs, not all at one time, but divide them and repeat the same procedure 2–3 times.
6. Arrange the watercress on a serving plate and place the meatballs on top. Serve with Szechuan peppercorns salt.

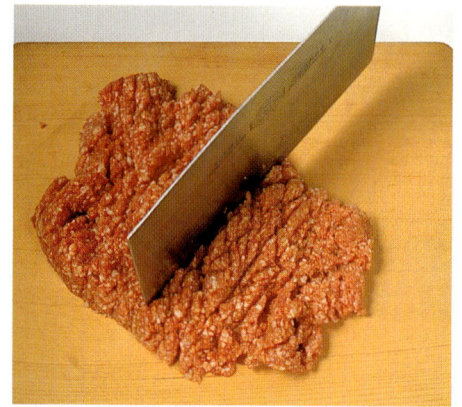

1

2

3

4

# Stir-Fried Lamb with Bean Paste

**Ingredients:**
450 g (1 lb.) lean lamb loin
1/2 egg white
2 teaspoons corntarch
Mixture A:
    1 1/2 tablespoons "tien-mien-chiang"
      (sweet brown bean paste)
    1 tablespoon sugar
    1 tablespoon soy sauce
    1 tablespoon cornstarch
3 cloves garlic
3 tablespoons sesame oil
Chinese parsley for garnish

**Method:**
**1.** Cut the lamb into thin slices (1), place in a bowl and combine with the egg white and cornstarch with your hands.
**2.** Heat 6 cups oil in a wok over medium-low heat. Add the lamb and quickly deep-fry for 1–2 minutes.
**3.** Combine mixture A well.
**4.** Slice the garlic.
**5.** Heat 3 tablespoons sesame oil in a wok, quickly sauté the garlic. When it becomes fragrant, add the lamb. Season with mixture A and stir-fry. Serve hot. Garnish with Chinese parsley. (2–4)

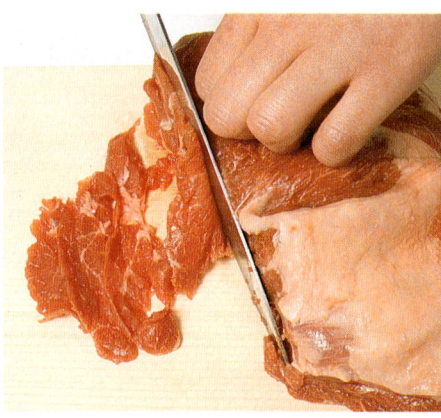
1

2

3

4

# "Ma-P'o-Tou-Fu"

**Ingredients:**
2 cakes tofu [in Japanese]: "tou-fu"
  [in Chinese] (bean curd)
  (500 g; a little over 1 lb.)
1 tablespoon "tou-chi" (fermented
  black soy beans)
1 red pepper
1 teaspoon minced garlic
1 tablespoon minced green onion
1 teaspoon minced fresh ginger
150 g (1/3 lb.) ground pork
1 tablespoon Chinese rice wine or sake
Seasoning Mixture:
  1/3 cup soup stock
  2 tablespoons sugar
  2 tablespoons soy sauce
  1 tablespoon "tien-mien-chiang"
    (sweet brown bean paste)
  1 teaspoon "tou-pan-chiang" (brown
    bean sauce)
  1/4 teaspoon salt
1 teaspoon cornstarch dissolved
  in 2 teaspoons water
2 tablespoons oil

**Method:**
**1.** Cut tofu into 1/2-inch (1 cm) cubes and let sit for a while to remove excess water.
**2.** Mince "tou-chi."
**3.** Seed the red pepper and cut into round slices.
**4.** Combine Seasoning Mixture well.
**5.** Heat 2 tablespoons oil in a wok over high heat and sauté garlic, green onion and ginger. When the fragrance is released, add the "tou-chi" and ground pork. Stir-fry.  (1–2)
**6.** Add tofu, Seasoning Mixture, and red pepper. Sprinkle with wine (3–4). Cover with a lid and cook over low heat for 15 minutes. Thicken with dissolved cornstarch.

1

2

3

4

# Braised Tofu with Chinese Mushrooms

**Ingredients:**
2 cakes tofu (bean curd)
   (250 g; 1/2 lb.)
8 dried Chinese mushrooms
   (smaller size)
1 head lettuce
For cooking lettuce:
   1 teaspoon salt
   1 cup water
Sauce Mixture:
   2 tablespoons soy sauce
   2 tablespoons soup stock
   1 tablespoon oyster sauce
   1/4 teaspoon sugar
2 teaspoons cornstarch dissolved
   in 4 teaspoons water
4 tablespoons oil
6 cups oil for deep-frying

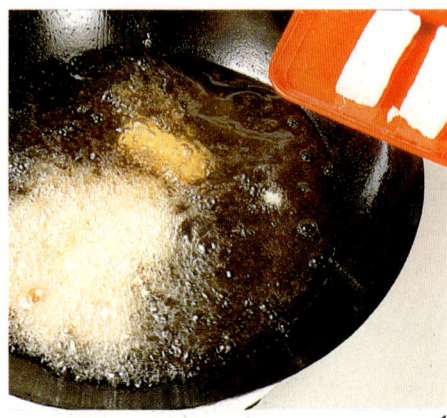

**Method:**
1. Cut tofu into 1-inch (2.5 cm) slices. Wipe each slice with a cloth or paper towel. Heat 2–3 cups of oil in a wok and deep-fry the tofu until golden brown. (1)
2. Soak mushrooms in water for 30 minutes. Drain and stem. (2)
3. Wash the lettuce. Heat 2 tablespoons oil in a wok and sauté the lettuce. Add salt and water, cover with a lid and cook until soft. Drain and place on a serving plate. (3)
4. In the wok heat 2 tablespoons oil and sauté the mushrooms and tofu. Add the Sauce Mixture and thicken with dissolved cornstarch. (4)
5. Place on the lettuce.

# Creamed Eggplants

**Ingredients:**
4 eggplants (American size)
4 cups thin soup stock (2 chicken cubes dissolved in 4 cups water)
Cream Sauce:
   1/2 teaspoon salt
   1/2 cup soup stock
   1/2 cup milk
   1/8 teaspoon pepper
2 teaspoons cornstarch dissolved in 4 teaspoons water
2 ham slices, minced for garnish

**Method:**
**1.** Wash eggplants, stem and peel. Cut lengthwise into 6–8 wedges (1–2). Soak in water for a while to remove harshness.
**2.** Cook eggplants in soup stock. Drain and place on serving plate. (3)
**3.** Heat the ingredients for the Sauce Mixture and thicken with the dissolved cornstarch. (4)
**4.** Pour the sauce over the eggplants and garnish with minced ham.

1

2

3

4

# Sautéed "Ch'ing-kêng-ts'ai"

### Ingredients:
500 g (a little over 1 lb.) "ch'ing-kêng-ts'ai" (green vegetable, see page 4)
1 teaspoon salt
1 cup water
2 tablespoons oil

### Method:
**1.** Wash "ch'ing-kêng-ts'ai" and cut crosswise into two parts, to separate the leaves and stalks. Cut the stalks lengthwise into thin slices. (1)
**2.** Heat 2 tablespoons oil in a wok. Sauté the sliced stalk, and then add leaves. Add salt and water, cover with a lid and cook until soft (2–4). Drain and serve on a plate.

Note: Spinach or snow peas may be substituted for "ch'ing-kêng-ts'ai."

# Vegetable Salad, Szechuan Style

**Ingredients:**
200 g (7 oz.) fillet of chicken breast
1 tablespoon Chinese rice wine or sake
1/4 teaspoon salt
100 g (3 1/2 oz.) ham
2 cucumbers
2 stalks celery
50 g (2 oz.) carrots
150 g (1/3 lb.) bean sprouts
1/2 head lettuce
10 g dried agar threads
Dressing:
   5 tablespoons soy sauce
   2 tablespoons vinegar
   1 1/2 tablespoons sugar
   1 teaspoon "tien-mien-chiang"
     (brown bean sauce)
   2 teaspoons red pepper powder
   1–2 teaspoons "chih-ma-chiang"
     (sesame seed paste)

**Method:**
**1.** Sprinkle the chicken with 1 tablespoon sake and 1/4 teaspoon salt, and steam or cook in an electric range. Shred into thin slices.
**2.** Cut ham, cucumbers, celery, lettuce and carrot julienne style. (1–2)
**3.** Wash bean sprouts and drain. Boil briefly.
**4.** Rinse agar threads and cut into 2-inch (5 cm) lengths. (3)
**5.** Mix dressing ingredients well and cool. (4)
**6.** Place some of lettuce on a large serving plate. Mix other ingredients and place on lettuce. Pour dressing over all.

1

2

3

4

# Pickles, Cantonese Style

**Ingredients:**
8–10 servings
2 cucumbers
1 cauliflower
1 lemon slice
4 green peppers
2 sweet red peppers
1 papaya
1 carrot
Vinegar Mixture:
  2 cups vinegar
  1–1 1/2 cups sugar
  1 teaspoon salt

**Method:**
1. Cut cucumbers into rolling cubes.
2. Boil cauliflower with lemon and break into bite-sized pieces.  (1)
3. Cut green peppers into two lengthwise, seed and cut into bite-sized pieces.
4. Cut the sweet red peppers the same way as the green pepper.
5. Peel papaya and cut into bite-sized pieces.
6. Peel carrot and cut into bite-sized pieces.
7. Boil vinegar in a small pan, add sugar and salt.
8. In a bowl place the carrot, green and red peppers and pimentos, and pour in the vinegar mixture (2). Let sit overnight.
9. Add the cucumber, papaya and cauliflower. Let sit four more hours and serve.

1

2

# Fried Rice with Pineapple

**Ingredients:**
3 cups rice, washed
1 pineapple
4 dried Chinese mushrooms
150 g (1/3 lb.) roasted pork
150 g (1/3 lb.) shrimp
2 eggs
1/3 cup frozen peas
Seasonings:
  1 teaspoon salt
  2 teaspoons curry powder
  2 tablespoons soy sauce
  1 tablespoon Chinese rice wine or sake
  Dash of pepper
4 tablespoons oil

**Method:**
1. Cook the rice with 3 1/2 cups water.
2. Cut the pineapple crosswise one-third from the top. Cut the inside away from the shell carefully. Then cut the removed part into 1/2-inch (1 cm) cubes. Set the pineapple shell and 1 cup of the pineapple cubes aside. (1)
3. Soak dried Chinese mushroom in water for 30 minutes and drain. Cut into 1/2-inch (1 cm) squares. Cut roasted pork into 1/2-inch (1 cm) cubes. (2)
4. Shell the shrimp, remove veins and wash.
5. Beat eggs in a bowl. Heat 2 tablespoons oil in a wok. Add eggs and fry quickly stirring constantly to get a fine texture.
6. Pour boiling water over peas and drain.
7. In a wok heat 2 tablespoons oil, sauté the shrimp and add pork, mushrooms, eggs, peas and pineapple. Mix in cooked rice and sprinkle with seasonings, mixing quickly over high heat (3–6). Fill the pineapple shell with the fried rice and serve.

1

2

3

4

5

6

# Rice Gruel with Chicken and Chinese Parsley

### Ingredients:
1 cup rice
   10–12 cups water
   1 teaspoon salt
   Dash of pepper
10 sheets of "won-ton" wrappings
1–2 chicken thighs with bones
   1/2 green onion
   1 clove of fresh ginger
   Little salt
   1–2 tablespoons Chinese rice wine or sake
Chinese parsley (fresh coriander)
Oil for deep-frying

### Method:
**1.** Rinse the rice. In a large thick pan cook the rice with 10–12 cups of water over high heat until it comes to a boil, and then reduce the heat. Cook about 1 hour.
**2.** Deep-fry the "won-ton" wrappings until light brown and flake into small pieces. (1–2)
**3.** Pull off the soft ends of the Chinese parsley for garnishing. (3)
**4.** Before steaming the chicken, rub it with salt and place on plate with the green onion and crushed fresh ginger. Sprinkle with wine (4). Place the plate in a steamer and steam for 15 minutes. (5 minutes if in a microwave oven). Dice into 1/2-inch (12 mm) cubes.
**5.** When the rice gruel is cooked, add salt and pepper to taste and serve with the chicken and Chinese parsley.

# Meatball Stew

**Ingredients:**
400 g (14 oz.) ground pork
1 teaspoon salt
1 tablespoon cornstarch
1/2 cup water
1/2 Chinese cabbage
For Soup:
    4 cups soup stock
    2 teaspoons sugar
    1 tablespoon Chinese rice wine
      or sake
    2 tablespoons soy sauce
2–3 tablespoons oil
6 cups oil for deep-frying

**Method:**
**1.** Pound the pork with the sharp edge of a knife to smooth the texture.
**2.** Wash Chinese cabbage thoroughly, cut into 2-inch (5 cm) lengths and drain. (1)
**3.** In a bowl combine the pounded pork, salt, cornstarch and water well until the meat becomes sticky.
**4.** Form into 2-inch (5 cm) sized meatballs with hands, throwing a portion of meat against each palm to extract air from the inside. (2)
**5.** Heat 6 cups of oil in a wok. Add meatballs and deep-fry over high heat 180°–190°C. (360–370°F.) until light brown. Drain. (3)
**6.** Clean wok. Heat fresh 2–3 tablespoons oil and sauté Chinese cabbage until soft. (4)
**7.** Remove Chinese cabbage to pottery casserole or deep, heavy saucepan, place meatballs on Chinese cabbage and pour in ingredients for soup. At first cook over high heat.
**8.** When the soup comes to a boil, skim scum, reduce heat, cover and simmer for an hour.

Note: If cooked in a pottery casserole, the stew may be served in the same casserole. If transferred to a serving bowl, the bowl should be warmed beforehand.

1

2

3

4

# Spring Rolls

**Ingredients:**
10 sheets spring roll skins
150 g (1/3 lb.) roasted pork
4 dried Chinese mushrooms
1/2 bundle scallions
300 g (2/3 lb.) bean sprouts
Seasoning Mixture:
    2 tablespoons soup stock
    1 tablespoon oyster sauce
    1 tablespoon soy sauce
    1 teaspoon sugar
    1 teaspoon salt
    Little sesame oil
2 teaspoons cornstarch, dissolved in 4 teaspoons water
2 tablespoons flour mixed with 3 tablespoons water to form a thick paste
4 tablespoons oil
6 cups oil for deep-frying

**Method:**
**1.** Cut the roasted pork julienne style. Soak the dried mushrooms in warm water for 30 minutes, remove stems and slice thinly. Wash and cut scallions into 2-inch (5 cm) lengths. Wash bean sprouts and remove black sprout shells and roots.
**2.** Heat 2 tablespoons oil in a wok and sauté bean sprouts and scallions. Remove from heat.
**3.** Heat 2 tablespoons of fresh oil in a wok, mix in and sauté the pork and mushroom, then add the cooked bean sprouts and scallions (1). Add the Seasoning Mixture. When it begins to a boil, thicken with the dissolved cornstarch. Divide the filling into 10 portions. Place each portion on a skin and brush the edge with the flour paste. Roll up and seal with the flour paste. (2–4)
**4.** Heat 6 cups oil in a wok on medium-high heat. Add the spring roll. Deep-fry and stir occasionally until golden brown (5). Remove and drain on paper towels.

Note: Enough dissolved cornstarch should be added to make the filling thick enough to stay inside the skins.

1

3

2

4

5

# Almond Gelatin Dessert

8–10 servings

**Ingredients:**
2 sticks dried agar
5 cups water
1 2/3 cups sugar
1 can (170 g: 6 oz.) evaporated milk
1 teaspoon almond extract
For Syrup:
   2 cups sugar
   2 cups water
12 strawberries
2 kiwi fruit
1 can (175 g: 6 oz,) mandarin oranges
1 banana

**Method:**
**1.** Wash dried agar and squeeze.
**2.** Tear agar into coarse pieces and boil with 5 cups water until completely dissolved. Stir in sugar until dissolved (1–2).
**3.** Wet a flat container and pour agar into the container, using strainer.
**4.** Add the evaporated milk and almond extract, mix, and set aside until cold (3). Chill in the refrigerator.
**5.** Boil 2 cups water and 2 cups sugar in small pan. Chill in the refrigerator.
**6.** Cut the chilled jelly into diamond shapes with a rounded knife (4). Remove to a serving bowl.
**7.** Wash the strawberries. Peel the kiwi fruit, cut lengthwise into two and then 1-inch (2.5 cm) slices. Drain mandarin oranges. Peel the banana and cut into bite-sized pieces. Place all the fruit pieces over the jelly and pour as much syrup as you like into the bowl.

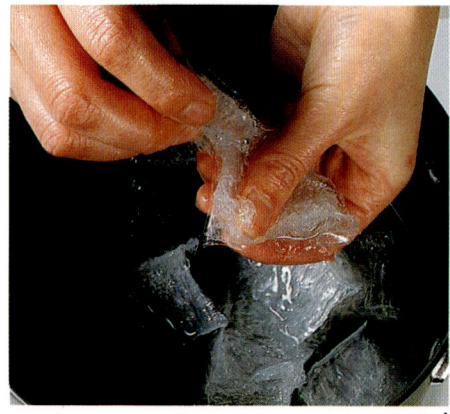
1

2

3

4

# Coconut Milk with Tapioca

8–10 servings

**Ingredients:**
1 cup dried tapioca
3 cups milk
1 cup coconut milk
1 cup sugar
1 teaspoon vanilla extract

**Method:**
**1.** Boil tapioca in pan until soft. Drain (1–2).
**2.** Combine milk with coconut milk. Add sugar and mix until smooth. Then add vanilla extract.
**3.** Add tapioca (3). Cool and serve.

1

2

3

# Pancake with Date Paste

**Ingredients:**
1 cup flour
2 eggs
2 tablespoons sugar
1 teaspoon vanilla extract
1 cup milk
600 g (1 1/3 lb.) dried dates
   2 cups sugar
   2 tablespoons lard or shortening
2 tablespoons oil

**Method:**
**1.** Beat eggs and mix with sugar, flour and milk little by little to make a smooth pancake batter. Add the vanilla extract.
**2.** In a pan cook the dates (with water) until soft. Strain through a sieve to get a smooth filling. Mix the paste thoroughly with sugar and lard. (1–2)
**3.** Heat the oil and fry 1 ladleful of batter at a time to make thin pancakes. Set aside.
**4.** On one pancake sheet put some of the date filling and spread it over the pancake. Then cover with another pancake sheet. (3)
**5.** Heat 2 tablespoons oil in a wok and slide the pancakes in from the edge of the pan. Fry until light brown, turn over and fry the other side (4). Remove from the oil. Cut the fried pancakes into desired sizes and serve.

# Menus for Special Occasions

Appetizers, pages 78–79.

Dinner Party, pages 80–81.

Simple Recipes, pages 82–83.

Bean Curd Recipes for Health, pages 84–85.

Noodle Recipes, pages 86–87.

Cooking at Table, pages 88–89.

Desserts, pages 90–91.

## Appetizers

Top Right: Fried Peanuts, page 96.
Left: Tossed Cucumbers, page 96.
Bottom: Hors d'Oeuvres, pages 94–95.

**Dinner Party**

Top Right: Beef and Tomato Soup, page 97.
Left: Braised Pork with Fermented Bean Curd, page 99.
Middle: Scallop Stew, page 98.
Bottom Right: Green Asparagus in Crabmeat Cream, page 100.
Left: Stir-Fried Prawns with Broccoli, page 101.

## Simple Recipes

Top Right: Celery Salad, page 105.
Left: Braised Fish Fillets, page 102.
Bottom Right: Stir-Fried Bean Threads, page 103
Left: Stir-Fried Beef with String Beans, page 104.

## Bean Curd Recipes for Health

Top Right: Braised Tofu, page 107.
Left: Tofu and "P'i-tan" Egg Salad, page 108.
Bottom Right: Sautéed Tofu with Crabmeat, page 108.
Left: "Tou-fu Chiao-tzu," page 109.

## Noodle Recipes

Top Right: Stir-Fried Cuttlefish with Vegetables, page 112.
Middle: Beef and Scallions with Stir-Fried Noodles, page 111.
Left: Fried Noodles with Shrimp, page 110.
Bottom Right: "Fried Noodle" with Crabmeat, page 114.
Left: Roast Pork with Noodles, page 113.

# Cooking at Table

Mongolian Fire Pot, page 88.

## Desserts

Top: Open Mouth Laughs, page 117.
Middle: Sesame Seed Balls, page 116.
Bottom: Steamed Cake, page 118.

## Preparation and Cooking...

Appetizers, pages 94–96.

Dinner Party, pages 97–101.

Simple Recipes, pages 102–105.

Bean Curd Recipes for Health, pages 106–109.

Noodle Recipes, pages 110–114.

Cooking at Table, page 115.

Desserts, pages 116–118.

# Appetizers

## "P'i-tan" Egg Custard

**Ingredients:**
3 "p'i-tan" eggs (thousand-year eggs)
5 eggs
Mixture A:
　1/2 cup soup stock
　1/2 teaspoon salt
　1/2 teaspoon sugar
Lard

**Method:**
1. Remove the clay from the "p'i-tan" eggs. Wash thoroughly and shell. Dice into 1/2-inch (12 mm) cubes. (1)
2. Beat the raw eggs gently to avoid air bubbles, combine with Mixture A and strain to obtain a smooth custard (2).
3. Thinly coat the inside of a shallow, oblong container with lard by hand, pour in the egg mixture, and put the diced "p'i-tan" eggs into the mixture (3). Bring water to a boil in steam cooker, and steam the mixture over low heat for about 20 minutes.
4. When the mixture is cooked, remove from the heat and cool. Cut the custard into two from the horizontally, then into slices 2 1/2–1/6 inch (7 cm–4 mm).

Note: This egg custard can be added to the assorted hors d'oeuvres shown in the picture. Place Vinegared Jellyfish with Cucumbers in the center of a serving plate and surround it artistically with the "p'i-tan" Egg Custard, Stir-Fried Prawns and Braised Chinese Mushroom.

## Braised Chinese Mushrooms

**Ingredients:**
5 dried Chinese mushrooms (large size)
Mixture A:
　1/3 cup soup stock or the leftover water used to soak mushrooms
　2 tablespoons soy sauce
　2 tablespoons sugar
　2 tablespoons Chinese rice wine or sake
　1/8 teaspoon salt
2 tablespoons oil
Few drops sesame oil

**Method:**
1. Soak mushrooms in water for 30 minutes, remove the stems and squeeze out the water.
2. In a wok heat 2 tablespoons oil, stir-fry the mushrooms until flavored and reduce the heat. Add Mixture A, cover with a lid and simmer. When the liquid is almost absorbed, sprinkle with sesame oil for flavor and glaze.
3. Cool and slice into 1/3–1/2-inch (8–12 mm) wide strips.

Note: Smaller ones may be served without cutting. This dish is usually added to the assorted hors d'oeuvres.

## Vinegared Jellyfish with Cucumber

### Ingredients:
200 g (7 oz.) dried, salted jellyfish, shredded
1 cucumber
Mixture A:
  4 tablespoons vinegar
  2 tablespoons soy sauce
  2 tablespoons sugar
  Pepper
Few drops sesame oil
Little mustard

### Method:
**1.** Soak the jellyfish in water overnight. Wash it and cut into 4-inch (10 cm) strings. Place it in a bowl and pour hot 50–60°C. (122–140°F.) water over it (1–2). When it has shrunk, remove it to cold water and drain.
**2.** Combine the jellyfish with Mixture A. Let stand for 20 minutes.
**3.** Cut the cucumber julienne style. Arrange the cucumber on a plate and put the jellyfish on top.

Note: If not already shredded, the jellyfish should be rinsed thoroughly to remove sand and dust after being soaked overnight, and then should be rolled up and cut into 1/8-inch (3 mm) wide strips.

For a variation, giant white radish can be substituted for the cucumber. Cut it julienne style and squeeze out the excess liquid. Combine vinegar, sugar, a little salt and sesame oil well. First marinate the jellyfish and then add the radish. As giant white radish is the main ingredient, jellyfish can be added as desired.

## Braised Prawns

### Ingredients:
300 g (10 oz.) prawns
1 tablespoon Chinese rice wine or sake
Mixture A:
  2 tablespoons Chinese rice wine
  1 1/2 tablespoons sugar
  1 1/2 tablespoons soy sauce
  1 tablespoon vinegar
  1 tablespoon tomato ketchup
  Little sesame oil
1 tablespoon ginger juice
Oil for deep-frying

### Method:
**1.** Trim off the legs of the prawns with scissors, wash and drain. Sprinkle with 1 tablespoon wine.
**2.** Pat the prawns dry with a cloth, and deep-fry.
**3.** In a wok bring Mixture A to a boil, add the ginger juice and quickly stir-fry the prawns in the sauce.

## Tossed Cucumbers

**Ingredients:**
4 cucumbers
1/2 carrot
Vinegar Mixture:
　4 tablespoons vinegar
4 tablespoons sugar
　1/2 tablespoon soy sauce
　Little sesame oil
Salt

**Method:**
1. Wash cucumbers and drain. Cut into rolling cubes. (1)
2. Shred the carrot.
3. Place the cucumber and carrot in a bowl. Sprinkle with salt. Let sit for a while until slightly soft. Pour in 1 cup water to remove the salt, and drain (2).
4. Mix the Vinegar Mixture in a bowl. Marinate the cucumbers and carrot. Toss occasionally and let sit for 15 minutes before serving.

## Fried Peanuts

**Ingredients:**
Fresh peanuts
Oil for deep-frying

**Method:**
1. Shell the peanuts and remove the thin skin.
2. Heat a large quantity of oil over medium heat, and deep-fry the peanuts. When the color begins to change, quickly remove them from the heat.

1

2

# Dinner Party

### Beef and Tomato Soup

**Ingredients:**
150 g (1/3 lb.) sliced beef
2 small ripe tomatoes
2 eggs
1 slice fresh ginger
Mixture A:
   2 tablespoons soy sauce
   1 teaspoon sugar
   1 tablespoon cornstarch
   2 tablespoons oil
6 cups soup stock
Dash of pepper
2 tablespoons oil

**Method:**
**1.** Cut beef into bite-sized pieces and marinate in Mixture A. (1–2)
**2.** Blanch and peel tomatoes, and cut into bite-sized pieces.
**3.** Beat eggs.
**4.** In a wok heat 2 tablespoons oil and sauté the ginger. Add the marinated beef.
**5.** Bring the soup stock to a boil in a pan and add tomatoes. When it begins to boil again, reduce the heat, add the beef and gradually pour in the beaten eggs. Add pepper to taste.

1

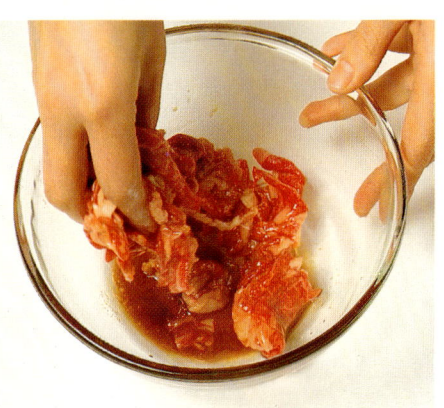

2

# Scallop Stew

**Ingredients:**
3 dried scallops
1 giant white radish
4 cups soup stock
1/4 teaspoon sugar
1 tablespoon Chinese rice wine or sake
Salt to taste
1 teaspoon cornstarch
   dissolved in 2 teaspoons water

**Method:**
1. Soak dried scallops in water overnight. Tear into pieces. (1)
2. Scoop out balls of white radish with a scoop or a tablespoon. (2)
3. Place the radish balls and scallops in a pan, pour in 4 cups of soup stock, and add sugar and wine. Cook over low heat for about one hour until the radish balls are tender. Add salt to taste.
4. Thicken with dissolved cornstarch and serve in a bowl.

1

2

## Braised Pork with Fermented Bean Curd

### Ingredients:
800 g (1 2/3 lb.) pork spareribs
1 piece of fresh ginger, sliced
Mixture A:
  2 tablespoons "hung-fu-ju" (mashed red fermented bean curd)
  1 1/2 tablespoons "tien-mien-chiang" (sweet brown bean paste)
  2 tablespoons sugar
  1 tablespoon Chinese rice wine or sake
1 stalk parsley
2 tablespoons oil

### Method:
**1.** Cut the pork lengthwise along the ribs and then, if too long, cut crosswise into 2 or 2 1/2-inch (6 cm) lengths.
**2.** In a wok heat 2 tablespoons oil, stir-fry the ginger and add the pork. Stir-fry well over high heat.  (1–2)
**3.** Remove to pottery or deep thick pan and add Mixture A. Pour in enough water to cover the pork and cook over high heat. When it reaches the boiling point, reduce the heat and cook for 45 minutes, stirring occasionally as the "tien-mien-chiang" in the Mixture scorches easily. Place on a serving plate and garnish with parsley.

1  2

# Green Asparagus in Crabmeat Cream

**Ingredients:**
2 bundles green asparagus
1 can (93 g: 3 oz.) crabmeat
1 slice fresh ginger
1 teaspoon salt
1 cup water
2 cups soup stock
1 tablespoon Chinese rice wine or sake
Mixture A:
    1 cup soup stock
    1/4 teaspoon salt
    Dash of pepper
    Little sesame oil
1 teaspoon cornstarch
    dissolved in 2 teaspoons water
4 tablespoons oil

**Method:**
1. Wash green asparagus, remove tough stem ends and peel thinly. (1)
2. Take the crabmeat out of the can. Remove the bones and flake.
3. Crush the ginger slices with the side of a knife.
4. Heat 2 tablespoons oil in a wok over high heat, and sauté the asparagus. When the color turns bright, add salt and water, cover with a lid and boil quickly.
5. When the asparagus is almost cooked, remove from the heat and drain on a strainer.
6. In the wok bring 2 cups soup stock to a boil, add the asparagus and cook for 1–2 minutes and drain. Place on a serving plate.
7. Heat 2 tablespoons oil in a wok and then sauté the ginger. When it becomes fragrant, add the crabmeat, sprinkle with wine and season with Mixture A. (2)
8. When the liquid comes to a boil, thicken it with the dissolved cornstarch. Pour over the asparagus and serve hot.

Note: Boil asparagus without cutting. After being boiled, it can be cut into 2–3 pieces and served.

1

2

### Stir-Fried Prawns with Broccoli

**Ingredients:**
10–12 prawns
300 g (2/3 lb.) broccoli
3 slices fresh ginger
1 clove garlic
1 tablespoon Chinese rice wine or sake
Mixture A:
   1 tablespoon soup stock
   1 tablespoon oyster sauce
   1 teaspoon salt
   1/4 teaspoon sugar
   Little sesame oil
   Dash of pepper
   Dash of MSG
6 cups oil for deep-frying
3 tablespoons oil
Little salt

**Method:**
1. Shell prawns, leaving the tails. Slit lengthwise down the back of prawns, and devein. Cut off the tips of the tails, push out water from tails with dull edge of knife and wipe well with dishcloth.
2. Boil broccoli in a generous amount of water with a little salt, rinse in cold water and drain. Split into flowerets (1–3).
3. Mince the garlic. Crush the fresh ginger with the side of a knife. Combine Mixture A well.
4. Heat 6 cups oil in a wok and deep-fry the prawns. When they turn red, remove them from the oil quickly.
5. Heat 3 tablespoons oil in a wok and sauté the garlic and the ginger. When they becomes fragrant, add the broccoli and prawns. Sprinkle with wine. Pour in Mixture A and stir-fry quickly over high heat.

1

2

3

# Simple Recipes

## Braised Fish Fillets

**Ingredients:**
300 g (2/3 lb.) white meat fish fillets
Mixture A:
   1 tablespoon Chinese rice wine or sake
   1 tablespoon soy sauce
   Little sesame oil
For coating fish:
   1/2 egg, beaten
   Cornstarch
1–2 chives for garnish
Mixture B:
   1/3 cup soup stock
   1 teaspoon sugar
   1/4 teaspoon salt
   1/2 tablespoon soy sauce
6 cups oil for deep-frying

**Method:**
**1.** Remove the bones and skin from the fish fillets. Cut the fish into 1/2 to 1 1/2-inch (1 to 4 cm) rectangles and marinate in Mixture A for 10 minutes. (1)
**2.** Mince the chive. (2)
**3.** Coat the fish with the beaten egg and then dust with cornstarch. Heat 6 cups oil in a wok over high heat and deep-fry.
**4.** In a wok boil Mixture B and add the deep-fried fish. Reduce heat and simmer until the liquid is almost evaporated. Remove to a serving plate and sprinkle with the chopped chive.

1

2

## Stir-Fried Bean Threads

### Ingredients:
50 g (2 oz.) bean threads
1 chili pepper
2 tablespoons minced green onion
150 g (1/3 lb.) ground pork
Mixture A:
    2 1/2 tablespoons soy sauce
    1 teaspoon sugar
    1 teaspoon "tou-pan-chiang" (brown bean paste)
    1 tablespoon Chinese rice wine or sake
2 tablespoons oil

### Method:
**1.** Pour boiling water over the bean threads and cut into 4-inch (10 cm) lengths. (1)
**2.** Cut the chili pepper into 1/5-inch (5 mm) round slices.
**3.** In a wok heat 2 tablespoons oil and stir-fry the green onion and pork, then add the bean threads (2). Season with Mixture A and mix well.

1

2

## Stir-Fried Beef with String Beans

**Ingredients:**
200 g (7 oz.) sliced beef
Mixture A:
    2 teaspoons sugar
    2 tablespoons soy sauce
    2 teaspoons cornstarch
    2 tablespoons oil
300 g (2/3 lb.) string beans
1 teaspoon salt
1 cup water
1 teaspoon minced garlic
1 teaspoon minced fresh ginger
1 tablespoon Chinese rice wine or sake
Dash of pepper
4 tablespoons oil

**Method:**
**1.** Cut the beef into bite-sized pieces, and marinate in Mixture A.
**2.** String the beans, cut into 2-inch (5 cm) lengths, and sauté in 2 tablespoons oil over high heat. Add the salt and water, cover and cook until soft (1–3). Drain.
**3.** Heat 2 tablespoons oil in a wok and sauté the garlic and ginger. Add the marinated beef and sauté until almost done. Finally add the string beans and sprinkle with wine and a dash of pepper.

1

3

2

# Celery Salad

**Ingredients:**
350 g (almost 3/4 lb.) celery
2 tablespoons black sesame seeds
Mixture A:
   1 teaspoon salt
   1/2 teaspoon sugar
   1 tablespoon soy sauce
   2 tablespoons sesame oil

**Method:**
**1.** Wash the celery and discard the stringy parts. Cut lengthwise into 2-inch (5 cm) pieces and slice thinly. (1)
**2.** Toast the sesame seeds. (2)
**3.** In a bowl combine Mixture A well, and add celery and sesame seeds. Toss briefly and remove to a serving bowl.

1

2

# Bean Curd Recipes for Health

## Tofu and "P'i-tan" Egg Salad

### Ingredients:
1 1/2 cakes tofu (bean curd)
1 "p'i-tan" egg (thousand-years egg)
1 stalk Chinese parsley (fresh coriander)
2 tablespoons minced green onion
1 teaspoon salt
1 teaspoon sugar
1 teaspoon sesame oil

### Method:
**1.** Wrap the tofu with a cloth to remove excess water, and crumble coarsely in a bowl. (1)
**2.** Remove the clay coating the "p'i-tan" egg. Wash thoroughly and shell. Dice into 1/5-inch (5 mm) cubes.
**3.** Cut the Chinese parsley julienne style.
**4.** Add the egg, Chinese parsley, and green onion to the crumbled tofu (2–3).
**5.** Mix salt, sugar, and sesame oil, and season the ingredients in the bowl. Serve in a bowl and garnish with Chinese parsley.

Note. "P'i-tan" eggs are often purchased in plastic packages. They should be kept in a well-ventilated container at home.

1

3

2

## Braised Tofu

### Ingredients:
2 cakes tofu (bean curd)
1 bunch spinach
   1 teaspoon salt
   1 cup water
Mixture A:
   1/3 cup oyster sauce
   1 teaspoon sugar
   1 tablespoon water
   1 tablespoon Chinese rice wine or sake
   Little sesame oil
Oil for deep-frying

### Method:
**1.** Cut the tofu crosswise into 1/2-inch (12 mm) slices. (1)
**2.** Wash the spinach thoroughly and drain.
**3.** Combine Mixture A well.
**4.** Wipe off water from the tofu and deep-fry until light brown. (2)
**5.** In a wok heat 2 tablespoons oil and stir-fry the spinach over high heat. Add salt and water, cover with lid. Cook until soft and drain.
**6.** In the wok bring Mixture A to a boil and cook the deep-fried tofu until the sauce is almost absorbed.
**7.** Place the spinach on a plate and arrange the tofu on top.

1    2

# Sautéed Tofu with Crabmeat

**Ingredients:**
2 cakes tofu (bean curd)
1 can (105 g) crabmeat
2 tablespoons minced green onion
1 tablespoon Chinese rice wine or sake
1 tablespoon soy sauce
1 teaspoon sugar
1/2 teaspoon salt
2 tablespoons soup stock
2 teaspoons cornstarch dissolved in 4 teaspoons water
2 tablespoons oil

**Method:**
1. Remove the bones from the crabmeat and flake it.
2. Cut the tofu lengthwise into four rectangles and slice into 1/3-inch (7 mm) pieces (1). Allow it to sit on the cutting board for 15 minutes.
3. Heat 2 tablespoons oil in a wok and sauté the green onion. Add the crabmeat and sprinkle with wine.
4. Add the tofu and season with soy sauce, sugar and salt. Pour in the soup stock. (2)
5. Cover with a lid and cook for a while. Thicken with dissolved cornstarch.

1

2

## "Tou-fu Chiao-tzu"

1 dozen

**Ingredients:**
1 cake tofu (bean curd)
50 g (2 oz.) ground pork
50 g (2 oz.) shelled shrimp
Mixture A:
  1/2 teaspoon salt
  1 teaspoon Chinese rice wine or sake
12 pieces of 6-inch (15 cm) square gauze
Mixture B:
  1 cup soup stock
  1/2 teaspoon salt
  Little sesame oil
  Dash of pepper
  1 tablespoon Chinese rice wine or sake
2 teaspoons of cornstarch dissolved in 4 teaspoons water
Little minced ham
Chinese parsley (fresh coriander) for garnish

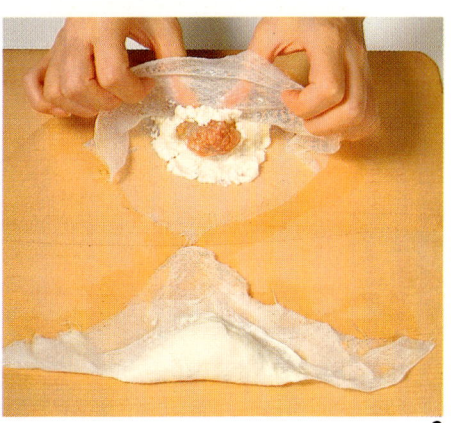

**Method:**
1. Cut the tofu in half lengthwise and then into 6 slices. (1)
2. Shell the shrimp, devein, and wash. Drain well and grind with a mortar and pestle.
3. In a bowl mix the ground pork and the shrimp. Season with Mixture A and make 12 meatballs.
4. Place one piece of the tofu in the middle of a square piece of gauze, mash the tofu with fingers to make a paste. Put a meatball on top of the paste and gather up the ends of the gauze so as to wrap the meat ball filling with the tofu paste. Make into a crescent shape as you do with "chiao-tzu." (2)
5. Steam the "tou-fu chiao-tzu" wrapped with the gauze in a steamer for 10–12 minutes. When cooked, remove the gauze and arrange on a plate.
6. Bring Mixture B to a boil in small pan, thicken with dissolved cornstarch and pour over the "tou-fu chiao-tzu." Sprinkle with minced ham.
7. Garnish with Chinese parsley (fresh coriander).

# Noodle Recipes

### Fried Noodles with Shrimp

**Ingredients:**
200 g (7 oz.) shrimp
1/2 egg white
2 teaspoons cornstarch
100 g (3 1/2 oz.) "tou-miao"
　(pea sprouts)
4 packages Chinese noodles
Sauce Mixture:
　1 cup soup stock
　2 tablespoons soy sauce
　1 tablespoon Chinese rice wine or
　　sake
　1/8 teaspoon sugar
　Little sesame oil
2 teaspoons cornstarch dissolved
　in 4 teaspoons water
5–6 tablespoons oil
Oil for frying

**Method:**
**1.** Shell the shrimp and remove the veins. Wash thoroughly and wrap with a cloth to remove the excess water.
**2.** In a bowl squeeze the egg white with your hands to get a smooth texture. Mix the shrimp with the egg white, add 2 teaspoons cornstarch and mix thoroughly.
**3.** Heat 6 cups oil in a wok over medium heat and deep-fry the shrimp until almost cooked. Set aside.　(1–2)
**4.** Wash the "tou-miao" and remove the tendril.
**5.** Bring a generous amount of water to a boil in a large pot and boil the noodles briefly. Thoroughly rinse and drain.
**6.** Heat 3–4 tablespoons oil and sauté the noodles until light brown. Remove to individual plates.
**7.** Heat 2 tablespoons oil, sauté the "tou-miao" add the shrimp and season with the Sauce Mixture (3). Thicken with dissolved cornstarch. Pour over the fried noodles.

1

3

2

## Beef and Scallions with Stir-Fried Noodles

**Ingredients:**
150 g (5 oz.) sliced beef
Mixture A:
  2 teaspoons sugar
  2 tablespoons soy sauce
  2 tablespoons oil
  2 teaspoons cornstarch
100 g (3 1/2 oz.) scallion buds
4 packages Chinese noodles
Mixture B:
  1/2 cup soup stock
  1 teaspoon sugar
  1 tablespoon soy sauce
2 teaspoons cornstarch dissolved
  in 4 teaspoons water
4 tablespoons oil

**Method:**
**1.** Cut beef into bite-sized pieces and marinate in Mixture A. (1)
**2.** Cut scallion buds into 2-inch (5 cm) sections. (2)
**3.** Prepare Stir-fried Chinese Noodles as explained on page 110 (directions 5 and 6).
**4.** In a wok heat 2 tablespoons oil and stir-fry the beef. Set aside.
**5.** Heat 2 tablespoons oil in a wok, stir-fry the scallion buds, add the beef, and season with Mixture B (3). Thicken with dissolved cornstarch. Pour this mixture over the stir-fried noodles.

1    2

3

# Stir-Fried Noodles with Cuttlefish and Vegetables

**Ingredients:**
1 cuttlefish
100 g (3 1/2 oz.) boiled bamboo shoot
2 large dried cloud ears
100 g (3 1/2 oz.) snow peas
1 teaspoon salt
1 cup water
4 packages Chinese noodles
Mixture A:
   1 cup soup stock
   1/2 teaspoon salt
   1/8 teaspoon sugar
   1 tablespoon Chinese rice wine or
     sake
   Dash of pepper
   Little sesame oil
2 teaspoons cornstarch dissolved
   in 4 teaspoons water
8 tablespoons oil

**Method:**
1. Gut the cuttlefish and remove the skin. Score the surface with crisscross cuts, then cut into bite-sized pieces. (1)
2. Cut the bamboo shoot into bite-sized wedges. (2)
3. Soak the cloud ears in water, remove the stems and cut into bite-sized pieces.
4. String the snow peas (3). Heat 2 tablespoons oil, and stir-fry them. Add salt and water, cover and cook until soft. Drain.
5. Prepare Stir-fried Chinese Noodles as explained on page 110 (directions 5 and 6).
6. In a wok heat 2 tablespoons oil, stir-fry the cuttlefish and set aside.
7. In a wok heat 2 tablespoons oil. First stir-fry the bamboo shoot and the cloud ears. Then add the cuttlefish and the snow peas. Season with Mixture A and thicken with dissolved cornstarch. Pour over the stir-fried noodles.

1

3

2

## Roast Pork with Noodles

### Ingredients:
4 packages Chinese noodles
300 g (10 oz.) bean sprouts
1/2 bunch of scallions
4 dried Chinese mushrooms
150 g (5 oz.) roast pork
Mixture A:
    1/2 cup soup stock
    1/4 teaspoon sugar
    1/4 teaspoon salt
    1 teaspoon soy sauce
    Little sesame oil
    Dash of pepper
2 teaspoons cornstarch dissolved
    in 4 teaspoons water
6 tablespoons oil

### Method:
**1.** Prepare Stir-Fried Chinese Noodles explained on page 110 (directions 5 and 6).
**2.** Rinse the bean sprouts. Cut the scallions into 2-inch (5 cm) sections (1).
**3.** Soak the dried mushrooms in water for 15 minutes and squeeze out water. Remove the stems, and slice thinly.
**4.** Cut the roast pork into thin slices and then into strips.
**5.** In a wok heat 2 tablespoons oil and stir-fry the bean sprouts and scallions. Set aside.
**6.** In the wok heat 2 tablespoons oil and stir-fry the roasted pork and the mushroom. Add the bean sprouts and scallion and season with Mixture A (2). Thicken with the dissolved cornstarch. Pour this mixture over the stir-fried noodles.

1    2

## Fried Noodles with Crabmeat

**Ingredients:**
1 can (93 g: 3 oz.) crabmeat
50 g (2 oz.) "jiu-huang"
  (yellow scallions)
200 g (7 oz.) boiled bamboo shoots
4 packages Chinese noodles
Sauce Mixture:
  1 cup soup stock
  1 teaspoon soy sauce
  1/8 teaspoon sugar
  1/2 teaspoon sugar
  1/2 teaspoon salt
  1 tablespoon Chinese rice wine or sake
2 teaspoons cornstarch dissolved in 4 teaspoons water
7–8 tablespoons oil

**Method:**
1. Remove the bones from crabmeat. Flake crabmeat coarsely.
2. Wash the "jiu-huang" and cut into 2-inch (5 cm) lengths. Slice thinly the bamboo shoots.
3. Prepare Stir-Fried Chinese Noodles as explained on page 110 (directions 5 and 6). (1–2)
4. Heat 2 tablespoons oil in a wok and sauté the leek briefly, add the crabmeat and stir-fry. Set the "jiu-huang" and the crabmeat aside in a wok to make a little space at the bottom of the wok, pour Sauce Mixture into the space. Bring Mixture to a boil and mix the crabmeat and the "jiu-huang" with Mixture.
5. Thicken with dissolved cornstarch and pour over the noodles.

1

2

# Cooking at Table

### Mongolian Fire Pot

**Ingredients:**
1 kg (2 lb.) lean lamb loin
1/2–1 Chinese cabbage
1 bunch spinach or chrysanthemum leaves
120 g (4 oz.) dry bean threads
8 fresh Chinese mushrooms
1 cake tofu (bean curd)
Seasoning for dip:
  1/4 cup minced fresh Chinese coriander
  1/4 cup minced scallions
  1/4 cup minced green onions
  1/4 cup "hong-fu-ju" (fermented bean curd)
  1/4 cup "Chih-ma-chiang" (sesame seed paste)
  1/2 cup Chinese rice wine or sake
  1/2 cup soy sauce
  1/4 cup brown sugar
  Vinegar/Oyster Sauce/Sesame oil
  Salt

1    2

**Method:**
1. Slice the lamb very thinly.
2. Wash the cabbage, cut into bite-sized pieces. Wash the mushrooms and remove stems. If using dried mushrooms, soak in water to soften. Wash the spinach, cut into 2-inch (5 cm) lengths.
3. Soak the bean threads in warm water for 10 minutes until soft. Drain and cut into 3-inch (7.5 cm) lengths.
4. Cut the tofu into bite-sized pieces.
5. Arrange the lamb, vegetables, bean threads and tofu on a plate.
6. Fill the fire pot or other earthenware casserole with water or soup stock. Bring to a boil, then add vegetables bean threads and tofu. Give each person a small bowl for mixing the sauce, as needed. Swish each piece of lamb through the soup, dip in the sauce and eat. (1–2)

# Desserts

## Sesame Seed Balls

16 balls

**Ingredients:**
For the dough:
   300 g (2/3 lb.: 10 oz.) "shiratamako"
     (high glutinous rice powder)
   1 cup sugar
   1 cup water
For Fillings:
   1/2 cup sugar
   1 cup water
   1/2 cup "sarashi-an" (sweetened
     powdered bean paste)
   2 tablespoons lard
   1/8 teaspoon salt
White sesame seeds for coating
Oil for deep-frying

**Method:**
1. To make the fillings, dissolve the sugar in water over low heat, add the "sarashi-an," stir in lard and salt and mix thoroughly. Let cool.
2. To make the dough, dissolve the sugar in water over low heat and remove from the heat to cool. Little by little pour the syrup into the "shiratamako" in a bowl and knead with the hands until it gets smooth and as soft as an earlobe. (1)
3. Divide the dough and filling into 16 portions. Shape each portion into a ball.
4. Flatten each portion of dough into a round 1 1/2 inches (4 cm) in diameter. Place each portion of filling on each portion of dough. Gather the edges and wrap and filling completely, shaping the ball with the palms of your hands. Coat with sesame seeds. (2–3)
5. Heat 6 cups oil to 120°C. (250°F.) and turn off the heat. Put the sesame balls into the oil and let stand for 5 minutes. Then turn on the heat again and roll the balls in the oil until the balls become evenly light brown, occasionally pushing the balls down with a ladle as the dough can easily puff up and break. (4)

1

2

3

4

## Open Mouth Laughs

3 dozens

**Ingredients:**
300 g (2/3 lb.: 10 oz.) flour
1 tablespoon baking powder
2 tablespoons lard or shortening
1 cup sugar
2 eggs
1 teaspoon vanilla extract
Water (1/2–2/3 cup)
White sesame seeds for coating
Sugar mixed with colored sprinkles
Oil for deep-frying

**Method:**
**1.** In a bowl sift the flour with baking powder. (1)
**2.** To the sifted flour add lard, sugar, egg, and vanilla extract. Mix with water little by little until the dough becomes as soft as an earlobe. (2)
**3.** Make the dough into 2-inch (5 cm) balls, and roll the balls in sesame seeds.
**4.** Deep-fry the balls over high heat until the balls begin to crack. Then reduce the heat and deep-fry over medium heat until golden brown. (3)
**5.** Serve on a plate and sprinkle with sugar mixed with colored sprinkles.

1

2

3

# Steamed Cake

**Ingredients:**
2/3 cup flour
1 tablespoon baking powder
5 egg whites
1 cup sugar
1 angelica or sugared lemon rind
1/2 cup raisins
Powdered sugar for frosting
Lard

**Method:**
**1.** Mix flour with baking powder and sift.
**2.** Stiffly beat egg whites while gradually adding 1 cup sugar.  (1)
**3.** Slice the angelica or sugared lemon rind.
**4.** Mix the flour with the angelica and raisins and then with the beaten egg whites (2). Grease a cake pan with lard. Pour the mixture into the pan, and steam over high heat for 15–20 minutes.
**5.** Cut the cake into the desired sizes and sprinkle with powdered sugar.

1

2

# SOME USEFUL HINTS FOR COOKING

**"Ch'ao"** 炒 **(Stir-frying)**—The important thing is to do it quickly.

Stir-frying is a very common Chinese cooking method. When stir-frying, heat a small amount of oil to a high temperature, add the ingredients and stir and toss over high heat for a very short time.
1) Careful preparation is the key to success. Whether you are shredding or chopping the ingredients, cut them in pieces of uniform size and shape so that they can all be cooked in a short time and to the same degree. The vegetables must be thoroughly drained prior to stir-frying.
2) Some ingredients require seasoning before stir-frying. Thinly sliced meat or fish is marinated in seasonings. It is also important to measure and mix the necessary seasonings and spices and have them ready in a bowl.
3) When stir-frying different ingredients, you should first parboil or deep-fry those that take longer to cook. Marinated meat must be stir-fried first, then cooked with other ingredients.
4) Aromatic vegetables like green onion, garlic and ginger should be stir-fried until the oil is well flavored, before the rest of the ingredients are added.
5) Pre-heat wok, add oil and heat over high heat, then start with the ingredients that take the longest to cook. When using gas ranges with low heating power, pre-heat the wok thoroughly, or stir-fry half the amount of the ingredients at a time. In this way, the food will remain crisp and firm.

**"Cha"** 炸 **(Deep-frying)**—Be sure to use plenty of oil.

As using a lot of oil is thought to be a characteristic of Chinese cooking, it is assumed that there are many deep-fried Chinese dishes. Actually, in many of the recipes, the ingredients are not just deep-fried, but first deep-fried and then stir-fried, stewed or covered with thickening.
1) All ingredients should be of approximately the same size and shape so that they can be evenly cooked. Meatballs or fishballs should also be of the same size, and should be deep-fried for an equal length of time.
2) Marinated ingredients should be placed on a skimmer and thoroughly drained, then wiped with paper towels to remove moisture before deep-frying.
3) Large fish or large pieces of meat must be deep-fried twice, because they tend to burn on the outside while the inside is still underdone, if you fry them at a high temperature. First deep-fry them at a low temperature, remove them from the oil, raise the heat to high and refry them until golden brown and crisp.
4) Oil can be recycled economically if you use it properly. Use fresh oil for deep-frying ingredients coated in egg white and cornstarch batter that should remain white when fried, or for crisp Spring Rolls. Then, use the oil for ingredients with ordinary egg-cornstarch coating. Finally, use it for deep-frying marinated ingredients.

**"Shao"** 燒 **(Stew)**—Careful preparation is the secret of delicious dishes.

In Chinese cooking, "shao" means to stew. "Hung-shao-p'ai-kuo" is Braised Pork in Thick Sauce, and "hung-shao-shih-tzu-tou" is Meatball Stew. See pages 36 and 66.
1) Use thick pots so that ingredients can be simmered slowly until their flavors are agreeably blended. Stew pots and earthenware pots are the most suitable. Ingredients cooked in earthenware pots keep warm long after they have been removed from the heat.
2) Stir-fry or deep-fry meat and fish before stewing. In this way, the ingredients will keep their flavor and their shape even when they have been cooked for a long time.

Meats and entrails must be thoroughly rinsed in water and parboiled before stewing to remove any unpleasant smell. Parboil the meat until its surface begins to change color. Drain blood from the entrails and rinse them in cold water before placing them in the pot with seasoning.
3) Carefully adjust the heat when stewing. Place the ingredients and the seasonings in the pot, add water just to cover, put on the lid and cook, first over high heat until it starts to boil, then reduce the heat and allow it simmer, skimming from time to time.

# Techniques

**"Chêng"** 蒸 **(Steaming)**—Adjust cooking time and heat to the ingredients.

Steaming is a very simple method of cooking: all you have to do is to place the ingredients in the steamer and steam. As a result, steamed ingredients keep all their natural taste, so that it is important to use only fresh ingredients, particularly when you are steaming fish.

1) Chinese style steamers are the most handy. The lid is netted with bamboo mesh so that the steam rises through the lid and the temperature is properly controlled.

2) Adjust the heat to the ingredients. Fish and "pao-tzu" (Chinese buns) should be steamed quickly at a high temperature, whereas Chinese egg custard should be cooked over low heat, because it will become porous when overcooked.

3) If you lift the lid too often, the temperature inside the steamer will drop so that the "pao-tzu" will stop rising and the taste of the fish will be spoiled.

4) When placing "pao-tzu" in a steamer, arrange them well apart because they will rise and swell when cooked. Coat the bottom of the steamer with oil or place "pao-tzu" or "shao-mai" on cabbage leaves to prevent sticking.

**"Liu, Hui"** 溜・燴 **(Thickening)**—Dissolve cornstarch in twice as much water.

In "liu" recipes, you either prepare a sauce thickened with cornstarch and cover the cooked ingredients with it, or cook and season the ingredients first and then add cornstarch dissolved in water at the last moment. Thickened dishes keep warm for a long time and are smooth and pleasant to the palate.

1) The ingredients used in Liu-Recipes should be seasoned beforehand and cooked by deep-frying, stewing or steaming.

2) Dissolve cornstarch, in twice as much water. When the thickening is too thin, the ingredients become watery; when it is too thick, it tends to curdle.

When adding dissolved cornstarch, adjust the amount according to the consistency of the sauce.

3) When you have added dissolved cornstarch, let it boil until the thickening becomes transparent. If you turn off the heat too early, the thickening will not be sufficiently smooth and may taste of uncooked cornstarch.

4) Serve thickened dishes in large bowls. Many of the thickened dishes are beautiful to look at and fit to be served at banquets so you must be careful how you present them. Small bowls overflowing with thickening do not look very appetizing.

**"Pan"** 拌 **(Mixing)**—Cut the ingredients into pieces of equal size and shape so that they absorb the flavor of the seasonings to the same degree.

In Chinese cooking, there are salads made with uncooked vegetables or with cooked and uncooked ingredients, and salads that are eaten hot or mixed while still hot but served cold. Served in small bowls or plates, many of them can be eaten as accompaniments for wines and spirits, as side dishes, or as substitutes for European-style salads.

1) Cut the ingredients in pieces of the same size and shape. This will not only make them look more appetizing, but also allow them to absorb uniformly the flavor of the seasonings.

2) Some salads taste better when mixed just before serving. You can cut the ingredients beforehand, but wait till the last moment to dress them. On the other hand, there are salads that require marinating. These should be prepared in advance and kept in the refrigerator. Stir and toss from time to time to ensure even flavoring.

3) Prepare the dressing in a separate bowl. Mix the liquid seasonings first, then add sugar and salt, so that these will dissolve better and in a shorter time.

4) When you are adding seasonings in paste form, such as "chi-ma-chiang" (sesame seed paste), "tou-pan-chiang" (brown bean paste), etc., it is easier to use an eggbeater.

## Index of Recipes

**Appetizers**
Hors d'oeuvres
   Braised Chinese Mushrooms, 78, 94
   Braised Prawns, 78, 95
   "P'i-tan" Egg Custard, 78, 94
   Vinegared Jellyfish with Cucumber, 78, 95
Spring Rolls, 68

**Eggs**
Egg Fu Yong, 25
Scrambled Eggs with Tomatoes, 27
Stir-Fried Pork with Cloud-ears, 26
Stir-Fried Shrimp and Eggs, 24

**Chicken**
Deep-Fried Curried Chicken, 30
Fried Chicken with Cashew Nuts, 32
Roast Chicken, Chinese Style, 34
Steamed Chicken with Hot Sauce, 18

**Fish and Shellfish**
Braised Fish Fillets, 82, 102
Fried Spicy Prawns, 28
Marinated Smoked Salmon and Turnips, 20
Scallop Stew, 81, 98
Stir-Fried Prawns with Broccoli, 80, 101

**Meats**
Beef and Tomato Soup, 81, 97
Beef in Oyster Sauce, 40
Braised Pork with Fermented Bean Curd, 80, 99
Deep-Fried Meatballs, 46
Fried Pork in Thick Sauce, 36
Pearl Balls, 42
Steamed Pork Loaf with Salmon, 44
Stir-Fried Beef with String Beans, 82, 104
Stir-Fried Lamb with Miso Paste, 48
Sweet-and-Sour Pork, 38

**Noodle Recipes**
Beef and Scallions with Stir-Fried Noodles, 87, 111
Fried Noodles with Crabmeat, 87, 114
Fried Noodles with Shrimp, 86, 110
Roast Pork with Noodles, 86, 113
Stir-Fried Noodles with Cuttlefish and Vegetables, 87, 112

**Tofu Recipes**
Braised Tofu, 85, 107
Braised Tofu with Chinese Mushrooms, 52
"Ma-P'o-Tou-Fu," 50
Sautéed Tofu with Crabmeat, 85, 108
Tofu and "P'i-tan" Egg Salad, 84, 106
"Tou-fu Chiao-tzu," 84, 109

**Vegetables**
Celery Salad, 83, 105
Corn Chicken Soup, 22
Creamed Eggplants, 54
Fried Peanuts, 78, 96
Fried Rice with Pineapple, 62
Green Aspragus in Crabmeat Cream, 81, 100
Pickles, Cantonese Style, 60
Rice Gruel with Chicken and Chinese Parsley, 64
Sautéed "Ch'ing-kêng-ts'ai," 56
Stir-Fried Bean Threads, 83, 103
Tossed Cucumbers, 78, 96
Vegetables Salad, Szechuan Style, 58

**Cooking at Table**
Meatball Stew, 66
Mongolian Fire Pot, 88, 115

**Desserts**
Almond Gelatin Dessert, 70
Coconut Milk with Tapioca, 72
Open Mouth Laughs, 90, 117
Pancake with Date Paste, 74
Sesame Seed Balls, 91, 116
Steamed Cake, 90, 118

## Ingredients, Seasonings and Spices

**Chinese Names**

Chiang (Fresh ginger root), 7
Chi-ma-chiang (Sesame seed paste), 10
Ch'ing-kêng-ts'ai, 5
Chiu-ts'ai (Scallion), 6
Chiu-ts'ai-hua (Scallion flower), 6
Fu-ju (Fermented bean curd cake), 11
Fên-p'i (Mung bean sheets), 8
Fên-ssǔ (Mung bean noodles), 8
Hai-chê-p'i (Jellyfish), 9
Hao-yu (Oyster sauce), 11
Hsia-mi (Dried shrimp), 8
Hsiang-ts'ai (Chinese coriander), 5
Hua-chiao (Szechuan peppercorns), 11
Huang-la-chiao (Red chili pepper), 8
Hung-tsao (Dried red dates), 9
Jiu-huang (Yellow scallion), 5
Kan-pei (Dried scallops), 9
La-yu (Chili pepper oil), 11
Mu-erh (Cloud ears), 8
Pak-choi, 7
P'i-tan (Thousand-year eggs), 8
Suan-miao (Garlic leaves), 6
Suan-tai (Garlic sprouts), 6
Ta-suan (Garlic), 6
Ta-ts'ung (Green onion), 7
Tien-mien-chiang (Sweet brown bean paste), 10
Tou-chi (Fermented soy beans), 10
Tou-miao (Pea sprouts), 7
Tou-pan-chiang (Brown bean paste), 10
Ts'ao-ku (Straw mushrooms), 9
Tung-ku (Dried Chinese black mushrooms), 9

**English Names**

Brown bean paste (Tou-pan-chiang), 10
Chili pepper oil (La-Yu), 11
Chinese coriander (Hsiang-ts'ai), 5
Chinese black mushrooms, dried (Tung-ku), 9
Chinese mushrooms, 7
Cloud ears (Mu-erh), 6
Dates, red, dried (Huang-tsao), 9
Fermented soy beans (Tou-chi), 10
Garlic leaves (Suan-miao), 6
Garlic sprouts (Suan-tai), 6
Ginger root (Chiang), 7
Green onion (Ta-ts'ung), 7
Jellyfish (Hai-chê-p'i), 9
Mung bean noodles, (Fên-ssǔ), 8
Mung bean sheets (Fên-p'i), 8
Oyster sauce (Hao-yu), 11
Pea sprouts (Tou-miao), 7
Scallion (Chiu-ts'ai), 6
Scallion flower (Chiu-ts'ai-hua), 6
Scallops, dried (Kan-pei), 9
Sesame seed paste (Chi-ma-chiang), 10
Shrimp, dried (Hsia-mi), 8
Straw mushrooms (Ts'ao-ku), 9
Sweet brown bean paste (Tien-mien-chiang), 10
Szechuan peppercorns (Hua-chiao), 11
Thousand-year eggs (P'i-tan), 8
Yellow scallion (Jiu-huang), 5